A QUEST FOR
GRANDEUR

A QUEST FOR
GRANDEUR

CHARLES MOORE AND THE
FEDERAL TRIANGLE

SALLY KRESS TOMPKINS

PHOTOGRAPHS BY JACK E. BOUCHER
OF THE HISTORIC AMERICAN BUILDINGS SURVEY

SMITHSONIAN INSTITUTION PRESS • WASHINGTON AND LONDON

Edited by Carolee Belkin Walker.
Production editing by Rebecca Browning.
Designed by Kathleen Sims.

Library of Congress
Cataloging-in-Publication Data

Tompkins, Sally Kress.
    A quest for grandeur: Charles Moore and the Federal Triangle /
Sally Kress Tompkins.
        p.   cm.
    Includes bibliographical references.
    ISBN 1-56098-161-X
    1. Federal Triangle (Washington, D.C.) 2. Public architecture—
Washington (D.C.) 3. Washington (D.C.)—Buildings, structures,
etc. 4. Moore, Charles, 1855–1942—Influence. 5. United States.
Commission of Fine Arts.   I. Title.
NA735.W3T65   1992
725'.1'09753—dc20   92–6574

British Library Cataloguing-in-Publication Data is available.

On the title page is a detail from one of the aluminum doors designed for the
entrances to the Justice Building by Paul C. Jennewein. The lions symbolize strength.

For permission to reproduce the illustrations appearing in this book, please
correspond with the owners of the works. The Smithsonian Institution Press does not
retain reproduction rights for these illustrations individually or maintain a file of
addresses for photo sources.
The photographs by Jack E. Boucher, pages 81–153,
are in the public domain and are part of the Historic American Buildings Survey
Collection, Prints and Photographs Division, Library of Congress. The photographs
on pages xvi and xix are reprinted courtesy of the Commission of Fine Arts.
Manufactured in the United States of America.

5 4 3 2 1
97 96 95 94 93
♾The paper used in this publication meets the minimum requirements of the
American National Standard for Permanence of Paper for Printed Library Materials
Z39.48-1984.

CONTENTS

FOREWORD

The role of Charles Moore in the development of the Federal Triangle is an attractive historical subject and a research opportunity, but over half a century passed without any claimant. When Sally Kress Tompkins answered, it was perfectly clear that her combination of historical scholarship and worldly pragmatism matched this subject. By that time, the topic had become largely forgotten, certainly neglected.

As Sally Tompkins's graduate studies adviser at George Washington University, I was less than enthusiastic when she first broached this subject to me. Charles Moore, member of the United States Commission of Fine Arts for thirty years and chair for twenty-two, himself would be more than sufficient for a graduate paper. Sally needed a canvas large enough to deal with Moore's rise to power and his recognition of a new and challenging theater in which to exercise it. He had all the elements of a distinctly Washington career.

The magnitude of the Federal Triangle project, far greater than the other federal building projects of the time period, attracted her. What convinced me that it was a good topic for Sally was the realization that without a problem of this magnitude, there would be no opportunity for Sally to explore the interaction between Charles Moore—the politician—and the planning of the Federal Triangle. Through Sally's efforts, I realized that without Moore there would have been no Triangle.

Tompkins had discovered an overlooked subject in Charles Moore and the Federal Triangle that she would follow through her academic career. The present work took form when she was appointed by the Dunlap Society to share her historical insight into the Federal Triangle for its project to publish, in microfiche form, the visual archives of Washington, D.C. By that time, Sally had realized that the guiding hand of Charles Moore was present at every turn of the development of the Federal Triangle.

Gen. William Tecumseh Sherman made the observation that "there is no limit to what a man can do if he will let someone else take the credit for it," and Charles Moore learned that essential lesson as secretary to Senator James McMillan of Michigan. From Detroit, one of America's great planned cities, the senator had learned about the City Beautiful movement, and Moore learned along with him.

The City Beautiful movement was born in 1893 at the World's Columbian Exposition. It was there that America, perhaps for the first time, saw the potential and beauty that unified design could bring to America's urban areas.

Primarily a planning movement, the City Beautiful movement affected many cities throughout the United States, but nowhere did it have greater impact and breadth than in Washington. And nowhere in Washington was it implemented more comprehensively than in the Federal Triangle.

Moore first sharpened his political spurs as secretary to Senator McMillan and as secretary to the Senate Committee on the District of Columbia. He crafted the Senate Park Commission and became its secretary and a principal author and editor of the McMillan Plan of 1901, which sought to establish the reinterpreted formal plan of Washington designed by L'Enfant. It was intended to achieve the neoclassical vision first seen in Chicago in 1893. The McMillan Plan viewed a Washington, D.C., that

would be formal and ceremonial, and although never officially approved, it had great influence over Washington during the next several decades.

Sally Tompkins's account begins with Moore's role as one of the authors of the 1901 plan. This was a work of enduring value that enlisted the loyalty, enthusiasm, and continuing support of its participants for their lifetimes. Among the participants were Daniel Burnham, a nationally recognized figure from his great success as executive architect of the Columbian Exposition, and Charles McKim, widely known and respected within the architectural profession. Frederick Law Olmsted, Jr., son of the founder of the landscape architecture profession in America, was responsible for much of the writing and illustrating of the committee's report. Moore and Olmsted wrote about and—in the case of Olmsted, illustrated—the designs of Burnham and McKim.

Never was a team so strongly presented and organized than this committee led by Charles Moore. He appears to have had no important part in the selection of the committee members, but from the first they commanded his deep respect. Moore traveled with them to the nearby capital cities of the young republic—Annapolis, Williamsburg—and then on an extended exploration of the Renaissance cities in western Europe. For Moore, this was educational as well as decisive in defining his service as political adviser to the three architects.

Charles Moore became the self-appointed guardian of the far-reaching and significant recommendations contained in the 1901 plan. He played the key role in such early battles as the location of the Department of Agriculture on the Mall, the location and design of Union Station, and the creation of the Commission of Fine Arts to provide the architectural review authority that institutionalized and put teeth in the McMillan recommendations.

From this beginning, as chairman, Moore promoted the commission to discreet but ever broadening dimensions of authority, from the design of federal buildings, to the design of adjacent buildings, and then to entire districts of the city. He supervised its relations with the National Capital Park and Planning Commission, the National Park Service, and other federal agencies with a large impact on the city of Washington.

The seven buildings that comprise the Federal Triangle represent the largest unified collection of Beaux Arts buildings in the world. Indeed, it was the culmination of the aesthetic movement that began at the Chi-cago World's Columbian Exposition. The unity of design over a large area achieved in Chicago in 1893 was also achieved in Washington, D.C., in the Federal Triangle, despite that individual buildings were the work of individual architects. At both the Chicago Exposition and the Federal Triangle, design rules were laid down to achieve a coherent unity—such as requiring uniform cornice and water-table lines. When the last of the buildings of the Federal Triangle was completed, the modern movement began its sweep across the American landscape. Now, fifty years later, it is time to reassess the design lessons of the Federal Triangle in particular and the Beaux Arts movement in general.

FREDERICK GUTHEIM

NOTE TO THE READER

This book is an examination of Charles Moore and his influence on the building of the Federal Triangle, perhaps one of the greatest accomplishments of the City Beautiful movement. It was written by Sally Kress Tompkins, my colleague and deputy chief of the Historic American Buildings Survey/Historic American Engineering Record (HABS/HAER), National Park Service, from 1983 until her death in 1989. This work is being published posthumously by her colleagues and friends. It is both a memorial to Sally Tompkins and one of her final contributions to her chosen field—historic preservation.

Although Sally completed this manuscript in 1976, she intended to update it to reflect the current developments in the Federal Triangle and then publish her manuscript. Her responsibilities at HABS/HAER and her early death precluded this, but the Commission of Fine Arts generously produced an epilogue to the book that brings the story of the Federal Triangle into the 1990s. The photographs, taken in 1991 by Jack Boucher, also present a current look at the Federal Triangle.

Compiling this book was the job of HABS/HAER staff member Caroline Russell Bedinger and Smithsonian Institution Press acquisitions editor Amy Pastan. I would like to express my gratitude to them and to all who helped in the publication of the book, especially Sally's children, Alicia, Ben, and Ted, who gave their permission to publish the manuscript and otherwise provided encouragement.

In her career, Sally contributed much to HABS/HAER and to the historic preservation movement. I invite you to sample the pleasures of Charles Moore's vision and its accomplishment, the Federal Triangle, through Sally's work and the writings of Frederick Gutheim, Charles Atherton, and Sue Kohler, and through the architectural photographs of Jack Boucher.

ROBERT J. KAPSCH
Chief, Historic American Buildings Survey/
Historic American Engineering Record

PREFACE

One cannot study the development of the city of Washington in the twentieth century without realizing the key role played by the Commission of Fine Arts. The commission provides an edifying example of the influence an institution can have in the formation of the urban landscape. From 1915 to 1937, the power wielded by the commission was closely connected to its chairman, Charles Moore. As the commission's leader and spokesperson and its only lay member, Moore both molded and reflected its stands. While Moore's power was dependent on his position as chairman of the commission, much of the commission's influence was based on Moore's personal prestige. The interrelation of the two is so great that one cannot be studied during this period without studying the other.

The commission's role in influencing the face of monumental Washington was multifaceted. The Public Buildings program initiated in 1926, which resulted in the development of the Federal Triangle, seemed to present the best vehicle for examining the power of the commission under the leadership of Moore. Interest in building the Triangle spanned the twenty-two years that Moore served as chairman, and in 1937, the year of Moore's retirement, the final Triangle building, the Federal Trade Commission, was being completed. The Triangle development occurred at a time when the commission was approaching the height of its powers while organizations that worked closely with it and shared similar aims, such as the American Institute of Architects and the Committee of 100, were either in a period of reduced prestige or pursuing other goals.

Much of the influence of Moore and the commission upon the Triangle was direct, documented by letters, reports, and newspaper accounts, but some of it was indirect and more difficult to demonstrate. An accurate assessment of the commission's influence requires a thorough understanding of its power, prestige, and goals. The early part of this work is devoted to a study of the antecedents, genesis, composition, and early history of the Commission of Fine Arts as well as a close look at the views and philosophy of Charles Moore, for these are what gave the commission its standing and allowed it to dictate the form of the Public Buildings program in the 1920s.

There have been no critical studies of the Commission of Fine Arts, nor any that recognize and document the power and influence of Charles Moore. Moore's relatively recent exit from the Washington scene may partially account for this. Several tributes by close associates and an occasional reference in a book on a related subject giving weight to his contribution encouraged further research, and active scholars in the field of Washington history generally agree that Moore's influence was very great indeed.

John Reps, in his book *Monumental Washington,* while not exploring Moore's influence in any way, does draw heavily on Moore's writings for his study. Joanna Zangrando's dissertation, *Monumental Bridge Design in Washington, D.C., as a Reflection of American Culture, 1886–1932,* which gives an interesting insight into Moore's influence on that structure, is the only study I have found that gives a fair assessment of Moore's power. [No new studies have appeared in recent years.]

The majority of my research was in the *Records of the Commission of Fine Arts* at the National Archives, the *Records of the Public Building Service* at the Washington National Records Center in Suitland, Maryland, and the *Charles Moore Papers* at the Library of Congress. Moore believed in keeping records and was a prolific author of books, articles, speeches, and letters. His unpublished *Memoirs,* copies of which are in the *Records of the Commission of Fine Arts* and the *Charles Moore Papers,* are a rich repository of material and enlarge upon his earlier statements in regard to many facets of the commission's work.

A QUEST FOR
GRANDEUR

Portrait of Charles Moore by Eugene Francis Savage, courtesy of the Commission of Fine Arts.

INTRODUCTION

The growing municipal reform movement at the turn of the century sparked an interest in the artistic development of the city. The World's Columbian Exposition of 1893 in Chicago provided a model for cities throughout the country, and the desire to transform metropolitan cores grown dreary by unrelieved commercialism was turned into a quest for grandeur. A host of municipal art societies took the lead in beautifying public areas and in establishing art commissions, whose panels of experts were to resolve questions of what would and what would not make the visible city more pleasing. By 1900, Boston, New York, Baltimore, and Philadelphia had such commissions, and by 1925, they would exist in twenty-one cities throughout the nation. In Washington, D.C., the Commission of Fine Arts was established by Congress in 1910. Though given an advisory role, it grew, in the next thirty years, to be a powerful force in the development of the national capital. The commission directed location, style, and choice of architect for government buildings and monuments, and in 1930, its influence was extended to private-sector projects that bordered on federal land.

The commission had three major goals during this period: the orderly development of the city closely adhering to the Senate Park Commission Plan of 1901, the construction of buildings based on classical forms whose design expressed the values of beauty, dignity, and permanence, and the placement of responsibility for designing those buildings in the hands of the best architects available. The Senate Park Commission Plan, also known as the McMillan Plan (named after the chair of the commission, Senator James McMillan), aimed at restoring the design intentions of the L'Enfant Plan.

As guardian of the 1901 plan, perpetuator of classical architecture, and advocate for the architectural establishment, the commission, under the leadership of Charles Moore, enjoyed a high degree of success. Moore was a member of the commission from its inception in 1910 until 1940—a period of great building activity in the nation's capital—and for twenty-two of those years, from 1915 until 1937, Moore served as its chairman. He led a commission of men of similar tastes, background, and training, giving it a unanimity of opinion that allowed it to speak with a single voice—and that consistently increased its impact.

By 1926, when the federal public buildings program for the Federal Triangle was initiated, the commission, strengthened by victories in disputes over the Lincoln Memorial and the Arlington Memorial Bridge, was established as a major force on the Washington scene, and Moore himself was at the height of his prestige and ready to shape the program.

The commission sought to guide the Federal Triangle program along the lines of the 1901 plan, which itself was directly related to the World's Columbian Exposition. The Chicago fair had brought together the nation's leading architects, landscape architects, sculptors, and painters who created a group of elaborate neoclassical buildings, uniform in style and scale, designed to form a harmonious composition. The fair's designers drew heavily on the architecture of imperial Rome with variations inspired by classical Greece, Renaissance Italy, and neoclassical France. The total effect was grand, and it caught the imagination of a nation.

Fiske Kimball, writing over thirty years later, saw the effect of the fair as far-reaching:

The cumulative impression of the classic phantasm was overwhelming. The throng of visitors, many of whom were seeing large buildings for the first time, was deeply stirred by the ordered magnificence and harmony of the Court of Honor. The example of unified effort and effect, associated with classic forms in which it had been achieved, was stamped on the memory of the whole nation.[1]

This national enthusiasm for what came to be known as world's fair classicism swamped what Frederick Gutheim calls "a creative response to the new architectural opportunities inherent in the industrial revolution,"[2] which appeared in the last half of the nineteenth century.[2] "The issue," wrote Kimball, "whether function should determine form from within or whether an ideal form might be imposed from without, had been decided for a generation by a sweeping victory for the formal ideal."[3] The growing interest in improving the appearance of Washington found inspiration in the dazzling splendor of the fair composition. Cities throughout America planned civic or cultural centers that were classical in design and grouped around a mall or grand boulevard. While many of the plans were never completed, and today a lone city hall or courthouse remains the only manifestation of the great enthusiasm for building a fair in every city, the effect on the urban landscape and urban life was far-reaching. The movement encouraged a centralized city and directed energy and funds into handsome buildings and plazas at a time when cities had many other pressing needs. While mainly aesthetic, the City Beautiful movement was not, Mel Scott points out, entirely devoid of other concerns, such as municipal efficiency and economy. Civic leaders were quick to accept the proposition "that grandeur, convenience, and

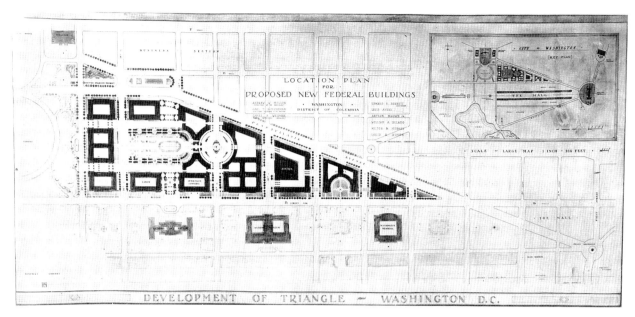

Early plan of the Federal Triangle by the Board of Architectural Consultants, 1927, courtesy of the Commission of Fine Arts.

View of the Federal Triangle from the Washington Monument in 1938, courtesy of the Commission of Fine Arts.

efficiency could be combined in a stately arrangement of public buildings."[4]

The great wave of neoclassicism set off by the world's fair was waning in other cities by the 1920s, as the public buildings program got under way in the nation's capital. Architects such as Louis Sullivan and Frank Lloyd Wright who sought designs indigenous to America and in keeping with its democratic ideals were still outside the mainstream and excluded from the big commissions, but their work was becoming noticed. Technological advances had made the use of classical forms in building seem structurally unnecessary, what Talbot Hamlin calls the "merest surface frosting." He pointed out that "the powerful scale of great Roman arches in steel-supported walls twelve inches thick was an obvious anomaly; and to surround steel frame members with the forms of the Doric or the Ionic or the Corinthian order seemed hardly less absurd."[5]

If arches and columns supported by steel and concrete seemed absurd, the inadequacies of the City Beautiful concepts of planning were becoming more serious and painfully apparent. Inadequate housing, neighborhood decay, and transportation problems plagued American cities. Enlightened civic leaders sought master plans for entire cities and their surrounding regions and the creation of regional planning commissions to control and regulate growth and alleviate the increasing social problems in urban areas.

In Washington, D.C., however, the artistic establishment dominated by the Commission of Fine Arts was successful in continuing to invoke the public buildings program to achieve the goals of the Chicago fair and the City Beautiful movement. In the years before the Public Buildings Act was passed by Congress in 1926, Moore and

members of the commission sought to ensure that federal buildings should be monumental as well as practical and located as proposed by the 1901 plan. In 1928, Congress authorized the purchase of all the land in the Federal Triangle, an area between the White House and the Capitol south of Pennsylvania Avenue and north of the Mall bounded by Fifteenth and Sixth streets. The Commission of Fine Arts saw here the opportunity to create a group of monumental buildings based on classical forms that related to one another harmoniously, according to the ideals of the Chicago fair. The construction of the much-needed government buildings was turned into a grand endeavor, and enthusiasm for making Washington the most beautiful capital in the world was widespread.

In spite of its advisory role, the Commission of Fine Arts under Moore's powerful leadership was able to dictate the form of the new buildings and the design of the Triangle. In successfully seeking revisions and modifications in the Triangle's design, the commission delayed certain aspects of its construction, and in the uncertain world of the 1930s, these delays proved costly. Criticism of classical eclecticism in architecture and City Beautiful planning, epitomized in the Triangle, became increasingly prevalent, and the aging Moore's faltering strength forced him to retire from the commission, weakening the strong organization he had forged. New Deal priorities brought the Triangle construction to a halt short of completion.

The commission's dedication to certain goals and its effectiveness in achieving them despite changing tastes were a result of its genesis, composition, and character, and of the personality and philosophy of Charles Moore, who was its most ardent advocate.

NOTES

1. Fiske Kimball, *American Architecture* (New York, 1928), 168.

2. Frederick Gutheim, *One Hundred Years of Architecture in America, 1857–1957* (New York, 1957), 11.

3. Kimball, *American Architecture*, 168.

4. Mel Scott, *American City Planning since 1890* (Berkeley, Calif., 1971), 43.

5. Talbot Hamlin, *Architecture through the Ages* (New York, 1940; 2d ed., 1953), 612–13.

CHAPTER I

THE 1901 PLAN

A t the end of the nineteenth century, a variety of persons and committees was responsible for the construction of new buildings and the erection of statues and monuments in the District of Columbia. The House and Senate Committees on the Library were responsible for statuary. The House and Senate Committees on Public Buildings and Grounds and the secretary of war, who served as general custodian of public lands in the District, were concerned with the construction and placement of federal buildings and monuments. Memorials were turned over to private groups or societies. Choosing architects, sculptors, planners, landscape architects was left to the discretion of the committee, official, or society involved, and each was free to choose the best available site without regard for any overall plan. The Commission of Fine Arts later commented that the result was a city lacking order and dignity and statues that "too often excited mirth rather than admiration."[1]

The circumstances surrounding the erection of a monument in honor of William Tecumseh Sherman in the 1890s, for example, drew national attention to the need for an art commission in the capital. The Sherman Memorial Commission ignored the decision of a panel of experts appointed by the National Sculpture Society, which judged the competition, and awarded first place to a design by Carl Rohl Smith, which the panel had not considered in the top four entries. The *New York Times* viewed the affair as an "outrage" and concluded that it was "about time the government provided the permanent art commission that has been proposed to pass upon statuary and pictures to adorn the national capital."[2]

The proposed art commission mentioned by the *Times* was promoted by the Public Art League of the United States, which had been formed by a group of American Institute of Architects (AIA) and Cosmos Club members in 1895.[3] They supported the creation of an art commission made up of a panel of experts to review buildings, sculpture, and paintings commissioned or acquired by the federal government. Their efforts in this direction proved futile. Had a fine-arts commission resulted from the Public Art League's proposal or from the controversy over the Sherman monument a year later, its composition, purpose, and character might have been quite different from the one that eventually took shape. The growing discontent of the period, however, found another outlet in the creation of a City Beautiful plan for Washington; it was to protect this plan that a fine-arts commission was eventually created.

Washington, D.C., was the City Beautiful movement's ideal city. The city's earliest buildings—its major edifices—the Capitol, the White House, the Treasury Building, were neoclassical in design, as was the city's original plan. The L'Enfant plan of 1791, originally designed by Pierre Charles L'Enfant and redrawn by Andrew Ellicott, however, had been too often ignored, its proposed vistas blocked. The rapid growth of the capital during the Civil War had prevented adhering to L'Enfant's plan and contributed to the disorder. Railroad tracks sprawled across the Mall, and the romantic gardens and winding paths designed by Andrew Jackson Downing filled another part of the Mall where L'Enfant had envisioned a formal composition.

The Washington centennial celebration in 1900 gave the Public Art League its chance to make its case. The American Institute of Architects' annual convention opened in the capital on the first day of the planned celebration. Glenn Brown, the AIA's secretary, arranged for papers presented at the convention to concentrate on the artistic development of the nation's capital. Brown had been active in the formation of the Public Art League and had recently published a book on the history of the United States Capitol. He had become interested in the L'Enfant plan and had been for some time a vocal critic of the quality of governmental art.[4] The architects had reason to be hopeful that there would be an enlarged role for the private architect in the designing of public buildings and monuments. The Tarnsey Act passed by Congress in 1893 had authorized the secretary of the Treasury to obtain designs by holding competitions, in which private architects would compete. Such competitions were not mandatory, however, and Secretary of the Treasury John G. Carlisle (1893–96) and Supervising Architect Jeremiah O'Rourke held none. In 1897, Lyman B. Gage, who had been president of the board of the Chicago Exposition, became secretary of the Treasury, and he elected to carry out the provisions of the act.

The papers on Washington solicited by Brown and delivered at the evening session of the AIA convention reflected optimism. The speakers pointed out the need for a comprehensive study and plan for the capital, urged the formation of a commission to advise the government on building sites, design, and models for public buildings and sculpture, and lauded the L'Enfant plan of the country's founding fathers. The architects demonstrated that they had learned the lessons of the Chicago fair, as they proposed buildings uniform in scale, broad terraces, balustrades, and reflecting water basins.[5]

Frederick Law Olmsted, Jr., suggested a return to the intentions of the L'Enfant plan for the Mall that simplified and unified the grounds between the Capitol and the monument. He envisioned a *tapis vert* similar to that at Versailles with parallel rows of trees, several pavements, and turf strips.[6]

Most of the papers presented concentrated on the development of the Mall and the grouping of public buildings, landscaping features, and statuary, but Paul Pelz, a member of the Washington Board of Trade, brought the vernacular city into the scheme. He pointed out that there was a strong movement started by the Board of Trade and supported by the local press for purchase by the federal government of that portion of the city bounded by Seventh, North B, and Fifteenth streets, south of Pennsylvania Avenue, an area that had deteriorated since the Civil War. This important location between the Capitol and the White House had been noted as a desirable site for future public buildings by other planners, including L'Enfant and more recently, Col. Theodore A. Bingham, the officer in charge of Public Buildings and Grounds, in the second of two plans he had prepared for the capital earlier that year.[7]

At the close of the convention, a special legislative committee was appointed to bring before the Congress a resolution calling for a commission to consider certain improvements in the capital. Charles Moore, then serving as secretary to James McMillan, an influential senator from Michigan, had followed the proceedings of the convention with interest, and he arranged for the AIA committee to meet with the senator, who chaired the Senate Committee on the District of Columbia. McMillan decided to take up the cause. In March of the following year at an executive session of the Senate he and

Moore, having tried various strategies, finally obtained passage of a bill that authorized the District Committee to employ experts to study the improvement of the District's entire park system. Expenses were to be paid from contingent funds of the Senate and overseen by the newly created Park Improvement Commission of the District of Columbia, to be commonly known as the Senate Park Commission or the McMillan Commission. Establishing the commission was an elaborate legislative maneuver; Moore and McMillan avoided the necessity of seeking the concurrence of the House or any conferences with other committees.[8] The AIA paid tribute to Moore's aid by noting in the proceedings of its convention the following year that Moore "took an active interest in the work, and through those devious ways, well-calculated to entangle our enthusiastic and trustful profession, he guided us safely to the first stage of success, and should have the sincere thanks of the Institute."[9]

Moore considered the Chicago world's fair, "the most momentous event in the history of the fine arts in America,"[10] and it seemed natural that he would select Daniel Burnham, president of the AIA in 1894, to head the Washington study.[11] McMillan wanted Frederick Law Olmsted, Jr., to serve as the commission's landscape architect; he had known Olmsted's celebrated father in connection with the designing of Belle Isle Park in Detroit. When Moore asked Burnham to chair the commission, Burnham inquired about the third member. Moore said the choice was up to him and Olmsted, but suggested Charles McKim. Burnham apparently welcomed the suggestion: Moore quoted him as saying McKim was "the man I had in mind. He was the one I most relied on in the Chicago fair work."[12]

The commissioners were men of proven expertise and experience. Burnham had been director of works for the Chicago exposition. McKim was the leading designer of neoclassical buildings in the country and had designed one of the buildings at the Chicago exposition. Frederick Law Olmsted, Jr., had worked with his father during the period that Olmsted, Sr., planned the landscaping of the fair buildings. Adding to the prestige of the commission was Senator McMillan, whose influence in Washington circles helped give the commission strong support. Perhaps his greatest contribution, however, was to lend the commission his efficient secretary, Charles Moore.

Moore was extremely knowledgeable about the District of Columbia. As clerk of the Senate Committee on the District, he had prepared reports for the improvements instigated under McMillan's chairmanship, including a study of the city water supply and the establishment of a new filtration system, the consolidation of the District's numerous streetcar companies, the reorganization of the city's charitable institutions, the elimination of grade crossings, and the extension of a highway system. Burnham wrote to a friend saying, Moore's "power is very great, although he keeps in the background."[13]

The tireless and confident Burnham, displaying the gift for organization that had made Chicago's Great White City on the shores of Lake Michigan a reality, began work on a plan for the capital city "on a scale," wrote Moore some years later, "which the wealth and taste of the country had come to demand and for which the fair had paved the way in the public mind."[14] Moore worked closely with the Senate Park Commission members—architects Daniel H. Burnham and Charles McKim, landscape ar-

chitect Frederick Law Olmsted, Jr., and, later, sculptor Augustus Saint-Gaudens—accompanying them on their seven-week trip to Europe. He used his journalistic experience to deal with the press, and stories regarding the commission's work were carefully timed to keep public interest whetted. He then joined Olmsted, Jr., to write the text of the report itself.

The report, complete with numerous photographs and maps, was submitted to the Senate Committee on the District of Columbia on January 15, 1902. It was a masterful piece of work meant to stir imaginations—which it did. That evening, a reception was held at the Corcoran Gallery of Art that featured two models: one of the city as it existed in 1901 and the other showing proposed changes. The models depicted an area of about two and a half miles from the Library of Congress to the proposed site for the Lincoln Memorial. Every public building was meticulously built in miniature, every private building outlined. The grades of streets and kinds of trees lining them were exact; more than five thousand photographs had been taken of buildings, streets, and city blocks to ensure accuracy. McKim had asked leading magazine illustrators to do paintings of his proposed designs for important buildings, monuments, and other structures, including the Lincoln Memorial and the Arlington Memorial Bridge.

McMillan called the plan "the most comprehensive ever provided an American city."[15] Compared with comprehensive city plans of today, the Senate Park Commission plan that dealt mainly with parks and the location, design, and landscaping of public buildings and monuments seems shortsighted; it ignored the business and residential areas of the city. Within those limitations, however, the report was as exciting as its creators had claimed. Their considerable talent and experience combined with a painstaking approach would give a new face to monumental Washington. Olmsted's park system extending to Great Falls and Mount Vernon restored to the city its regional setting. Olmsted also made provisions for new parks and for recreational facilities in Potomac Park.[16] It was the central composition, however, that captured the imagination of Washington and the nation. The Mall, cleared of railroad tracks and Downing's winding paths, was to become a green panel flanked by rows of elms. Shifted slightly south to restore the axial relationship between the Capitol and the Washington Monument, it now terminated at the proposed site for the Lincoln Memorial where the long sought-after Memorial Bridge would cross the Potomac. Public and semipublic buildings such as museums fronted on the Mall, and at its head was Union Square with statues of generals Grant, Sherman, and Sheridan replacing the botanical gardens. The design of Burnham's Union Station, with its dome sufficiently low to avoid rising above that of the Capitol, was part of the grand design. Buildings relating to the judicial and legislative branches were grouped around the Capitol, and those relating to the executive branch around Lafayette Square in proximity to the White House. B Street was extended so that it intersected with the diagonal Pennsylvania Avenue just east of Sixth Street, creating the triangle's angle opposite the western boundary at Fifteenth Street. The report recommended that the government purchase this area and suggested it include a hall of records, municipal buildings, and a modern market.

The report was well received by the press. The commissioners had been careful to enhance the prospects of the plan's acceptance by keeping key senators and congressional representatives well informed. McKim had sought the advice of Secretary of War Elihu Root, whose department had jurisdiction over the major portion of the public grounds, and he advised the commission not to stress any new aspects of its plans but to anchor them firmly in the past, presenting the scheme as a natural development of President Washington's plans for the capital.[17] The Senate Park Commission followed his advice, and while it was essentially new, they stressed the fact that it restored certain features of the L'Enfant plan. Supporters of the 1901 plan continued to use such phrases as "the plan of the founding fathers" and "the plan of Washington and Jefferson" to describe it, and not surprisingly, they fostered a receptive attitude in the patriotic climate of the times.

Opposition did arise—not to the plan itself but to its genesis and to the original formation of the commission, which had been created without House concurrence. Representative Joseph Cannon from Illinois, who was unalterably opposed to spending government money on art, also resented McMillan's high-handed methods. In 1903, he became Speaker of the House, a post he held for eight years and from which he battled against the plan.[18] As a result of opposition in the House, the plan as approved by the Senate was never adopted; during the next forty years, the various features would each be considered separately by Congress.

First to be tested in Congress was the change of location of the proposed railroad station. This bill passed Congress with McMillan's guidance on May 15, 1902. That August, McMillan died, and the major battle over the removal of the railroad tracks from the Mall, involving a large government expenditure to reimburse the railroad, had to be waged without him. Charles Moore remained in Washington after McMillan's death to push for its passage, which was finally won in February 1903. Cannon had bitterly opposed the measure, and Moore, writing in 1925, called its approval "the toughest of all."[19]

Moore then returned to Detroit and entered the business world as secretary of Union Trust Company. He would remain in business for fifteen years, but his life had been changed by his work with the Senate Park Commission, and he missed it. Moore had placed a high value on his close association with Burnham, McKim, and Olmsted. He had enjoyed the travel and the making of great plans, and he relished the working dinners at the Cosmos Club in Washington and at the Century Club in New York City where decisions regarding major projects were often reached. His friendship with Burnham and McKim would continue as long as they lived, and his loyalty to them as long as he lived. He wrote speeches and official letters for McKim[20] and, from 1906 to 1908, wrote the text for Burnham's plan of Chicago. His biographies of both men were published in the 1920s.[21] As Irving K. Pond correctly observed in his review of Moore's biography of Burnham, "His writing shows in what exalted esteem Mr. Moore held the man."[22] Another reviewer, Aymar Embury II, makes an even stronger commentary, stating that in Moore's volume, "Burnham figures as the perfect knight . . . a sort of architectural George Washington with a mouthful of aphorisms."[23]

The members of the Senate Park Commission had also returned to their separate cities, but they continued both individually and collectively to fend off challenges to the plan. Problems regarding the construction of the Department of Agriculture Building, which cut into the space reserved for the Mall, brought Burnham into conflict with Secretary of the Treasury Leslie M. Shaw and Secretary of Agriculture James Wilson. All the Senate Park Commission members came to Washington to testify in favor of legislation sponsored by Republican Senator Francis O. Newlands of Nevada prohibiting any building within four hundred feet of the central axis of the Mall.[24] The Senate Park Commission learned too late that the excavation for the Agriculture Building had established a ground level higher than suggested by the 1901 plan, and McKim was forced to seek President Roosevelt's personal intervention to rectify it.[25] The plan's creators agreed to try to anticipate problems, but their occupations continued to keep them in other parts of the country and made it difficult to remain in close contact with events in Washington.

Roosevelt, as a result of the furor over the Agriculture Building, appointed a consultative board made up of McKim, Burnham, Olmsted, and Bernard Green, superintendent of the Library of Congress. This informal board had no official status and did not help the Senate Park Commission anticipate challenges to the 1901 plan. It was indicative, however, of Roosevelt's general support.

The Senate Park Commission and the American Institute of Architects capitalized on Roosevelt's sympathetic attitude toward them by seeking a strong public statement from him in support of the plan, which he made in 1905 at the AIA's annual dinner. McKim and Glenn Brown gave careful attention to every detail—including a special train from New York for those attending from that city. Frank Millet, who was in charge of decorations at the Chicago fair,

personally planned and supervised the deco-
ration of the room at the Arlington Hotel
where the dinner was to be held. A special
box was built for Mrs. Roosevelt and her
friends when it was heard they would attend, and the gentlemen all stood up and applauded when they entered. President Roosevelt was one of the evening's speakers. His
speech answered their prayers:

> Whenever hereafter a public building is pro-
> vided for and erected, it should be erected in
> accordance with a carefully thought-out plan
> adopted long before, and it should not only be
> beautiful in itself, but fitting in its relations to
> the whole scheme of the public buildings, the
> parks, and the drives of the District.[26]

While Roosevelt's speech would be frequently quoted in defense of the plan of
1901 in years to come, it was Elihu Root's[27]
speech that set the tone not only for the
evening but for the future; it was filled with
the rhetoric that would be increasingly
employed by defenders of the 1901 plan.
He expressed reverence for the capital's
early architects who "take special merit
from their association with the founding
fathers . . . as men who gathered their inspiration not only from classic works of art, but
from love of country and the serene natures
of Washington and Jefferson." Referring to
the period after the Civil War, he said, "we
have passed through a dreadful time." Now,
however, "the lesson of the Chicago Exposition had gone into every city, town, and
hamlet of America . . . and our architects [at
the American Academy in Rome] can go directly to the source for their ideas of classic
art."[28] Discrediting buildings erected after
the Civil War and before 1900 and tying the
founding fathers to the neoclassicism of the
Chicago fair and the values of the American
Academy in Rome would remain a part of

the arguments in favor of the 1901 plan and
world's fair classicism for over a third of a
century.

The dinner was a glittering success.
More than $600,000 was raised for the
American Academy, and J. P. Morgan and
Henry Walters, who were in attendance,
were applauded when their individual contributions of $100,000 were announced.[29]
The evening was an example of what
McKim and his fellow architects could do
well; they were at home with men of wealth,
and they met with them frequently at private clubs to which they too belonged.[30]
The dinner, however, did not achieve a sig-
nal victory for the 1901 plan, which still had
to be fought out one battle at a time.

The conflict that arose two years later in
1907 demonstrated the deficiencies of Roosevelt's informal consultative board. The
1901 plan called for the Grant Memorial to
be one of the main features of the new
Union Square at the head of the Mall, a
scheme that involved relocating the botanical gardens. In 1903, when asked to judge
the competition for the Grant Memorial, the
members of the Senate Park Commission
had deliberately chosen a design suitable for
the head of the Mall. Preparation of the memorial site required destroying a number of
trees that had been planted as memorials. In
1907, William R. Smith, superintendent of
the botanical gardens, joined forces with the
major opponent of the plan in Congress,
Representative Cannon, to fight the proposed infringement. They enlisted the
newspapers on their side, and the *Washington
Post* of October 8 protested "that a government board proposes to substitute a panta-
looned statue for the living sculpture of
God."[31] When the controversy died down
and Congress and the papers alike grew
tired of eulogizing trees, the Grant Memo-

rial was fixed in accordance with the 1901 plan. Burnham, who had already threatened to resign from Roosevelt's consultative board, was disgusted. He wrote to Moore:

> What we need in Washington is a system . . . when work affecting our plan is afoot it should be someone's business to know about it and to promptly post all of us. As things are, one hears casually, when he hears at all, that something is happening, or has happened. [32]

Burnham would soon have his watchdog in Washington. Shortly before leaving office in January 1909, Theodore Roosevelt created by executive order a thirty-member Council of Fine Arts. He followed the guidelines suggested to him by an AIA delegation headed by Cass Gilbert. The council would be appointed by the president from a list of nominations made by the board of directors of the AIA. The supervising architect of the Treasury was to serve as executive officer. Roosevelt directed his cabinet to refer to the council for advice on architecture, selection of sites, landscaping, sculpture, and painting. The AIA quickly supplied a list of nominees, including all of the Senate Park Commission members (except Moore), and many Chicago fair artists. Roosevelt made the appointments, calling upon the new council to offer advice on the location and character of the Lincoln Memorial, currently a subject of congressional debate. The council held one meeting on February 10, 1909, before Roosevelt left office. It reported in favor of the location set by the Senate Park Commission. [33]

Congress resented Roosevelt's usurpation of its powers and refused to allow the council any appropriation for travel. When William Howard Taft took office in March, he revoked the executive order creating the council. Taft, however, was an advocate of

an art commission for Washington, and he sought the creation of such a commission through congressional channels. Elihu Root, now a senator, drew up the necessary legislation. Samuel McCall of Massachusetts guided the bill through the House, and it was signed by President Taft on May 17, 1910. The role of the commission was limited to an advisory one in connection with statues, fountains, and monuments; such limitations were necessary to secure its passage. [34] However, an important part of the act reads: "The commission shall also advise generally upon questions of art when required to do so by the President, or by . . . Congress." [35] This was used by President Taft in October 1910 when he extended the commission's influence by executive order stating that the plans for public buildings to be erected in the District of Columbia would not receive final approval until they had been submitted to the commission for its comment and advice. [36]

The commission was to consist of seven well-qualified judges of the fine arts who were to be appointed by the president for a period of four years each. Daniel Burnham was appointed to the commission and was elected its first chairman. Saint-Gaudens had died in 1907 and McKim in 1909, but Olmsted was made a member. Other appointees were connected by Chicago fair ties as well as personal ones. Daniel Chester French, the sculptor, had done a major work for the fair. Francis D. Millet, the painter, was director of decorations at the fair and a close friend of the other artists, especially Burnham. Cass Gilbert, architect and past AIA president, had served on the Jury of Fine Arts for the fair. Thomas Hastings, a partner in the notable firm of Carrère and Hastings, had contributed to the fair and served his apprenticeship at McKim, Mead, and White, where Gilbert had also apprenticed. The lay member was Charles Moore, the ardent admirer of the Chicago fair and secretary of the Senate Park Commission.

As Moore would later say with manifest understatement: "The plan of 1901 was placed in the hands of its friends."[37]

NOTES

1. Commission of Fine Arts, *Annual Report*, 1914 (Washington, D.C., 1914), 13.

2. *New York Times*, May 28, 1896.

3. The formation and work of the Public Art League of the United States are discussed in Glenn Brown, *Memories, 1860–1930* (Washington, D.C., 1931), 357–65.

4. Ibid., 207.

5. See Glenn Brown, comp., *Papers Relating to the Improvement of the City of Washington, District of Columbia* (Washington, D.C., 1901), especially Brown's own essay "A Suggestion for Grouping Government Buildings," which stresses the "delights of the L'Enfant Plan." See also in the same volume, H. K. Bush Brown, "Sculpture in Washington," which calls for maintaining the "plan of the founders," and George Oakley Totten, Jr., "Exposition Architecture in Its Relation to the Grouping of Public Buildings," which discusses the "lessons from Chicago."

6. Brown, comp., *Improvement*, 28–29.

7. See a discussion of Bingham's plans in John William Reps, *Monumental Washington: The Planning and Development of the Capital Center* (Princeton, N.J., 1967), 77.

8. Moore describes the events that led to the formation of the Senate Park Commission in his introduction to Brown's *Improvement*, 9; see also Charles Moore, ed., *The Improvement of the Park System of the District of Columbia* (Washington, D.C., 1902), 68–70.

9. American Institute of Architects, *Proceedings of the Thirty-fifth Annual Convention* (Washington, D.C., 1901), 46–47.

10. Charles Moore, "Personalities in Washington Architecture," *Columbia Historical Society Records* 37–38 (1937): 8.

11. Brown, *Memories*, 206–7; and Charles Moore, "The Government and the Practicing Architect," *Journal of the American Institute of Architects* 16 (March 1928): 90.

12. Charles Moore, *Daniel H. Burnham* (Boston, 1921), vol. 1: 137–39. Augustus Saint-Gaudens, the fourth member, was added at the request of Charles McKim in June 1901. His poor health limited his contribution to the commission, however.

13. Quoted in Thomas S. Hines, *Burnham of Chicago* (New York, 1974), 143.

14. Moore, "Personalities," 10.

15. "Report of the Senate Committee of the District of Columbia," in Moore, ed., *Improvement*, 16.

16. For a discussion of Olmsted's evolving concepts of city planning, see Mel Scott, *American City Planning since 1890* (Berkeley, Calif., 1971), 118.

17. A memo enclosed in Charles McKim to Daniel Burnham, August 28, 1901, Charles Moore Papers, Library of Congress, quoted in Reps, *Monumental Washington*, 104.

18. See Reps, *Monumental Washington*, 144; and Brown, *Memories*, 96–102, for a more extensive consideration of Cannon's influence and opposition to the 1901 plan.

19. Charles Moore to [?] Wheeler, 1925. *Charles Moore Papers*, Library of Congress.

20. Moore, *Burnham*, vol. 2: 60 n.

21. Moore, *Burnham*, vols. 1 and 2, published in 1921; and Charles Moore, *The Life and Times of Charles Follen McKim* (Boston, 1929).

22. Irving K. Pond, review of *Daniel H. Burnham*, by Charles Moore, *American Architect* (December 7, 1921): 417.

23. Aymar Embury II, review of *Daniel H. Burnham*, by Charles Moore, *Literary Review* (December 3, 1921): 222.

24. Moore, *Burnham*, vol. 1: 206–13. See also U.S. Senate Committee on the District of Columbia, *The Mall Parkway* (Washington, D.C., 1904).

25. Brown, *Memories*, 277–79.

26. Charles Moore, ed., *The Promise of American Architecture* (Washington, D.C., 1905): 18. The book contains the text of the addresses delivered that evening, and in his introduction, Moore describes the dinner. Brown outlines the preparations for the evening in *Memories*, 430–41.

27. Elihu Root, a cabinet member under both McKinley and Roosevelt, was a firm supporter of the 1901 plan. He served for many years as president of the Century Club in New York City and was a personal friend of many of the artists who were its habitués.

28. Moore, ed., *Promise of American Architecture*, 39, 40, 43.

29. Brown, *Memories*, 441.

30. McKim had also secured other notable speakers such as Jules Jusserand, French ambassador to the United States, James Cardinal Gibbons, and surprisingly, Joseph G. Cannon, Speaker of the House.

31. Quoted in Moore, *Burnham*, vol. 2: 23.

32. Ibid., 21.

33. Moore, *Burnham*, vol. 2: 120; Brown and Cass Gilbert petitioned Roosevelt for the council. See the text of the letters between the AIA and Roosevelt in Brown, *Memories*, 365–79.

34. Elihu Root to Commission of Fine Arts, April 22, 1935, on the occasion of its twenty-fifth anniversary: "If the bill had undertaken to give any compulsory effect to the opinion of the commission, it would not have passed." Reprinted in *Commission of Fine Arts Thirteenth Annual Report* (Washington, D.C., 1940).

35. *Public Law No. 181, H.R. 19962*. 61st Cong. 2d Sess. (May 17, 1910): 203.

36. *Executive Order 1259*, October 25, 1910.

37. Moore, *McKim*, 71.

CHAPTER II

THE EARLY YEARS OF THE COMMISSION OF FINE ARTS

It was evident from the time of the commission's formation that its first test would be the Lincoln Memorial. The memorial would anchor the 1901 plan by extending L'Enfant's central axis to an area beyond the Washington Monument in the newly created Potomac Park. The matter was a subject of debate in Congress. Representative Joe Cannon of Illinois strongly objected to the Potomac Park location, telling Elihu Root that as long as he lived he would never allow a memorial to Abraham Lincoln to be "erected in that God-damned swamp."[1] Other members of Congress favored a memorial highway stretching from Washington, D.C., to Gettysburg. Locations at the U.S. Soldiers Home, Meridian Hill Park, Arlington National Cemetery, and between the Capitol and Union Station were also being considered by Congress.

In February of 1911, Congress created the Lincoln Memorial Commission with the power to fix the location and choose the design. President Taft was named chairman, and Cannon was one of its members. At its first meeting, it requested the Commission of Fine Arts to report on the desirability of the various sites and to recommend the best method of selecting the memorial's architect and sculptor. While there was little doubt what a commission whose members were so overwhelmingly favorable to the 1901 plan would decide, the Commission of Fine Arts showed proper deliberation.[2] Moore and Francis D. Millet met informally with Daniel Burnham in Chicago for two days in April.

The report, written by Moore, recommended the Potomac Park site and, in a carefully worded passage, the type of designer.[3] Burnham, however, was adamant that the commission should go to Henry Bacon who had superintended McKim's buildings at the Chicago fair and on whom he felt that McKim's mantle had fallen. The Lincoln Memorial Commission accepted the Potomac Park location, and the commission recommended Henry Bacon. At Cannon's insistence, the Memorial Commission asked architect John Russell Pope to revise his designs for a memorial at the U.S. Soldiers Home for the Potomac Park site and submit them along with Bacon's designs for a final decision.

The Commission of Fine Arts recommended Bacon's design, which more closely followed that of McKim, but the matter was still undecided when Burnham left for Europe in 1912. Burnham had argued for Bacon in person before the Memorial Commission saying:

> The whole world is looking on and confidently expecting us to do something merely striking and picturesque and not notably ideal; . . . we must disappoint them and rise above their expectations as we did in Chicago in 1890. . . . Our whole standing in architecture and our influence on the taste and architectural judgment of the community are at stake in this matter.[4]

Francis Millet, returning from Europe just at the time that Burnham was crossing the Atlantic, went down on the Titanic; Burnham died suddenly ten weeks later at Heidelberg on June 1, 1912. The loss of the prestigious Burnham and the popular Millet was a staggering blow to the commission. In December, the Lincoln Memorial Commission selected Henry Bacon as the architect for the memorial. Moore felt the decision was an important one. He later wrote:

> The selection of Bacon as architect and the approval of his plans by the Lincoln Commission gave to the Commission of Fine Arts an established standing at this critical juncture, when

its usefulness was threatened by the loss of the potent leadership of Burnham and the mastery of Millet in dealing with the Washington situation.[5]

The Annual Report of the Commission of Fine Arts issued shortly before the memorial was completed called the choice of the Potomac Park location "a distinct victory for the Plan virtually insuring the realization of the large scheme as laid out in 1901."[6]

Daniel Chester French became chairman after Burnham's death, and Frederick Law Olmsted, Jr., succeeded Millet as vice chairman. President Taft, after consulting with commission members, named Edwin Howland Blashfield, the leading mural painter of the Chicago fair, to fill Millet's place on the commission and Peirce Anderson of Burnham's firm to fill Burnham's.

The sympathetic Taft was not reelected, however, and President Woodrow Wilson had no personal or political ties to the 1901 plan.[7] Wilson, according to both Glenn Brown and Charles Moore, was not interested in the artistic development of Washington. Brown, who was unable to obtain a personal interview with Wilson when he became president, stated emphatically: "He cared nothing for the fine arts and did not allow anyone to broach the subject to him."[8] Moore, in a tempered statement, wrote in his *Memoirs:*

> President Wilson received the members of the Commission in his White House office when they called officially on him soon after his inauguration in 1913. The cordial relations that through a dozen years had grown up with President Taft were not renewed during the eight years of the Wilson administration. The President was quoted as saying that when he looked from the windows of the White House what he saw was the hills of Virginia. His concerns

were strictly national until they became international.[9]

The commission, however, did not suffer during Wilson's administration. The officer in charge of Public Buildings and Grounds, who by law was the ex-officio secretary of the commission, was William W. Harts.[10] Harts enjoyed a close personal relationship with Wilson and was also a sympathetic supporter of the work of the commission. In 1913, Wilson extended the powers of the commission by ordering that all matters that affected in any important way the appearance of the city first be submitted to the Commission of Fine Arts.[11] Thus the commission enjoyed increased power in its first four years although its official role was advisory. The four-year report stated the commission's main goal was a "well and harmoniously developed capital."[12] It noted that the Potomac Park location of the Lincoln Memorial "completes the outline of a great plan according to the design of L'Enfant. The plan is to fill those outlines in harmonious fashion and at the same time to guard the city as far as possible from intrusion of high buildings and from unharmonious styles of architecture."[13]

Early in 1915, Daniel Chester French resigned from the commission to devote himself to the work on the statue of Lincoln for the memorial. The commission members then took what proved to be a very significant step—they elected Charles Moore as chairman.

Moore had assumed that Olmsted, the sole surviving Senate Park Commission member, would be the next chairman. In his *Memoirs*, he wrote that he was both surprised and reluctant to accept, feeling that an artist should lead the commission. However, Moore's personal life had undergone

changes that made his assuming the position appealing. Moore's wife of thirty-six years had died in 1914, and both of his sons were married and self-supporting. "It was no longer necessary," he wrote, "to pursue a business career," which he had been doing in Detroit for the previous twelve years. "After all the real interests in my life were in Washington. Now I was free to take on the increasing duties of the chairmanship, prolonging my monthly stay in Washington."[14]

Charles Moore stepped to center stage. As secretary to Senator McMillan, he had written reports and carried out improvement projects in the District but not in his own name. As secretary to the Senate Park Commission, he had put himself at the disposal of the artists, acting as their guide and publicist and finding ways to obtain the legislation, funds, and support they needed. He had enjoyed an intimate relationship with these artists, but he was in the background. Now as head of the Commission of Fine Arts, he would emerge as a powerful figure in his own right, although the cult of anonymity he had practiced for so long would still serve him in good stead. Congressmen, department secretaries, and presidents would take the bows. Moore would be content simply to have the matter decided as the Commission of Fine Arts had recommended.

Moore was sixty years old when he became chairman, a post he would hold for twenty-two years. In 1918, Moore finally moved to Washington and became acting chief of the Division of Manuscripts of the Library of Congress. But, in 1927, he would relinquish that post to devote himself full time to the commission's role in the public buildings program then getting under way in Washington—a program that in many ways proved a culmination of the power and influence of the commission under Moore's leadership.

Moore provided continuity as well as leadership throughout his chairmanship, molding as well as reflecting commission opinion. H. Paul Caemmerer, who served as the first civilian secretary of the commission from 1922 to 1954, in writing an article on Moore after his death, described him as "very modest in the presence of the artist members and [he] relied upon them for an interpretation of questions of art; yet they depended on Mr. Moore to carry out their ideas and had great respect for his judgement."[15] Moore himself saw his role as "the part of an appreciative layman among creative artists."[16] William Adams Delano, a prominent New York architect, who served as a member both of the Commission of Fine Arts and of the Board of Architectural Consultants,[17] interpreted Moore's role and paid him an elaborate tribute in an essay recalling Century Club architects:

> Charles Moore, for twenty-three years the guiding spirit of the Commission of Fine Arts in Washington, was so understanding of the architects and their point of view that he was their perfect mouthpiece, interpreting tactfully, sometimes forcibly, their decisions to Presidents, Senators and Congressmen. His task was not always easy but he performed it superbly. While he was chairman, he became as familiar a landmark as the Washington Monument. During the four years I served on the Commission, I came to have a great affection for him as a man, and unbounded admiration for the skill with which he drove his team of artists along the often rough road of contention. He had no special training in the arts and came to his position by way of his secretaryship to Senator McMillan's original Senate Committee which, under President Taft, became the Commission of Fine Arts. The orderly development of Washington was his passion for fifty years. He

wrote about Washington, talked about Washington and loved Washington. When he died in 1942, he had written many books on the history of the city and its builders. During his life he received well-deserved honors. If one had to name *the* man most responsible for the development of our present Capital, it would be Charles Moore.[18]

Moore was "the perfect mouthpiece" for the artists, but only for those artists who shared his artistic tastes; Moore had his own pronounced views on artistic matters and strong biases.

Moore had studied while at Harvard under Charles Eliot Norton whom he fondly termed "that belated Grecian."[19] He felt he owed to Norton's instruction and continued advice his "interest and pleasure in the work of the artist."[20] Moore particularly valued Norton's precept that architecture, sculpture, and painting "afforded evidence . . . of the moral temper and intellectual culture of the various races by whom they have been practiced."[21] Moore observed that "often one hears the objection that too much money is spent on fine work designed for all time, on good architecture where only shelter is needed. We are told that style should follow function. One admits that buildings and parks and monuments are but the setting for the life they serve."[22] Moore saw the national capital as "an outward and visible sign of the inward and spiritual grace of the Republic."[23]

To Moore, the answer to what was great architecture was found in the past, in the classical precepts of simplicity, proportion, dignity, and beauty. He weighed the merit of the work of the capital's earliest architects, all trained in the classical tradition. "The question is," he wrote, "do their buildings still live? The answer is: They do."[24] In defending the architecture of the Lincoln

Memorial, Moore pointed out "how shallow seems the criticism that a memorial designed on classic lines is unsuited to a man born in a log cabin, a splitter of rails, self-educated. . . . Fittingly Lincoln is commemorated by a form in which through the ages the mind and skill of man have found most complete expression."[25]

Moore's bias was apparent in his interpretation of the architectural history of the capital, a bias shared with the leadership of the American Institute of Architects and other proponents of the 1901 plan.[26] In speeches, articles, and reports Moore repeatedly traced the history of the capital and its buildings beginning with "the inherited tradition of Jefferson—the Greek orders"[27] and Washington's selection of L'Enfant, whose "genius consisted, as genius always does, in applying well-established principles of art to new situations and new requirements."[28]

Moore gave high ratings to James Hoban's White House and William Thornton's design for the Capitol, both based on classical precedents: "After the Revolution and down to the time of the Civil War, the American people were permeated with Greek and Roman ideals." The buildings then erected, the Treasury, the Patent Office, the Post Office [now the Tariff Commission Building] all were "carried out according to the great tradition established by Washington and Jefferson,"[29] Moore wrote. "The Civil War brought chaos in the arts. . . . Happily Washington building was at a standstill and so suffered little during this period."[30] During the Grant administration, "unfortunately the supervising architect was carried away by the 'modernism of his day' in building the State, War and Navy building [now the Old Executive Office Building] in the pseudo-classical style then popular."[31] The Pension Building was disdained: "Think

what would have happened if General Meigs [Montgomery Cornelius Meigs who designed the Pension Building] had not been rapped over the knuckles and made to let go his hold on the chief building of the nation."[32] The Library of Congress was criticized for its "ill-shaped dome, now happily well tarnished, that sought to outshine the dome of the Capitol itself. . . . Later the flames of Romanesque, or Richardsonesque, that swept the country like wildfire struck Washington in the guise of the city post office on Pennsylvania Avenue. Then, providentially the fire was arrested. The District building, the Natural History building, and the Department of Agriculture building showed a groping back towards the established order."[33]

By the end of the nineteenth century, according to Moore's scenario, things were changing for the better—partially as a result of the growing number of students training at the École des Beaux Arts in Paris and partially as a result of the World's Columbian Exposition. Moore described it this way:

> In 1893 the Chicago World's Fair changed the whole aspect of American civic life. On [the] sandy wastes of Lake Michigan's shore arose as if by magic a white city so harmonious in design, so highly developed in architectural treatment and landscape effects, so richly adorned with sculpture and painting that everywhere throughout the country admiration and emulation were universal. Washington was ready for the new order.[34]

Moore felt that the Senate Park Commission plan for Washington was "far in advance of public taste of that day. So they created the Commission of Fine Arts to watch over and protect those plans from such mutilations as the original plan, prepared under the inspiration and guidance of the fathers, had suffered."[35] Moore would generally conclude his histories with a list of the 1901 plan features that had been realized and then noted what remained to be done. He never neglected an opportunity to point out that those buildings that were not in the prevailing neoclassical style should be demolished.

> Thus from the beginning Washington was founded and has developed in an architectural fashion which belongs to the ages. Whatever has been the variations and departures elsewhere, in the main the national capital has been true to type, and the occasional yieldings to modernism in public buildings have served as warnings rather than as precedents. Today the aim is to rid the city of these excrescences.[36]

While Moore did have high regard for the opinions of artists, a term he applied to architects as well as sculptors and painters, he could only serve well those artists who shared his standards of taste. Moore represented the artistic establishment of the time, believing that great art must be rooted in the past and seeking classical precedents for important buildings. In particular, Moore spoke for the artists who marched under the banner of the Columbian Exposition and pledged allegiance to the 1901 plan.

Moore was also motivated by strong personal loyalties. His loyalty went first to Burnham and McKim, whom he perceived to be great artists, men of true genius. And Moore believed only men of genius should be chosen to design the nation's monuments.[37] In 1939, two years after his retirement, he wrote as well of his loyalty to the Senate Park Commission, the founding fathers, love of country, and the Commission of Fine Arts.[38]

Besides his own personal beliefs and loyalties, Moore brought other strong attributes to his post at the commission. He was dedicated and tireless and devoted a great deal of time to his nonpaying position. He was diplomatic in dealing with elected officials and appointed administrators, and willing to compromise. He enjoyed quoting a dictum of Charles McKim's that "one can compromise anything but the essence."[39] He had an intimate knowledge of Washington and its political workings. Moore also had the advantage of long tenure, giving him an advantage over recently appointed officials. He commented on this as early as 1923:

> The frequent changes in the officials charged with the conduct of affairs in the District of Columbia involve the necessity of newcomers becoming acquainted with the fact that there is [a] plan for the orderly development of the city of Washington, and this plan may not be departed from save at a permanent sacrifice of good order, convenience, and beauty.[40]

Moore eagerly took up the task of educating uninformed newcomers. His unwavering commitment to the 1901 plan and world's fair classicism and his zeal in arguing for them on nearly every occasion proved effective in maintaining their importance in the eyes of official Washington.

Moore possessed a high degree of administrative skill that was especially effective in bringing about agreement within the commission and making it an effective force in pursuing its goals. Matters regarding painting, sculpture, architecture, or landscape architecture were first taken up with those members of the commission who were experts in the field. This was usually done by letter between meetings or at social or club gatherings in New York. Opinions of past members in that field were also often sought. When the matter came up at the monthly meeting, uninformed members were presented with a fait accompli, with those commissioners who were experts in the field reporting on the matter one way or the other.

Moore also proved himself an able arbitrator. He recalled in his *Memoirs* a difference of opinion arising within the commission, an occurrence he termed rare. Past members were included in the meeting called to resolve the troublesome matter. Discussion begun in the morning was continued at lunchtime at the corner table at the Century Club and resumed back at John Russell Pope's office in the afternoon. Moore wrote:

> As the March twilight descended on Fifth Avenue all present had talked themselves into an agreement to carry out the Plan of 1901. . . . The physical strain in conducting such a meeting, seeing to it that each member had full opportunity to express his opinion and have it considered, is exhausting, even when the result, as in this case, was convincingly satisfactory to the chairman.[41]

While Moore proved an adroit manager in harnessing commission opinion behind the 1901 plan, his own power and influence were considerably enhanced by the fact that he led a unified and remarkably homogeneous commission. Moore quoted Andrew Mellon (Treasury secretary from 1920 to 1928) as telling him: "I like to get a report from the Commission of Fine Arts, for I know it is unanimous; not the result of compromise."[42]

The early commissioners shared standards of taste that related to the Columbian Exposition to which they had close ties. Later commissioners possessed common values based on similar backgrounds, education, and status. The commissioners individually would have agreed with Moore's evaluation of Washington architecture. They were all highly successful members of the artistic establishment. Oliver W. Larkin in his book on American art describes Daniel Chester French, sculptor of the Chicago fair, charter member of the Commission of Fine Arts and three years its chairman, as a man who "at fifty, with an income which one year reached eighty thousand dollars, lived in the world of good clubs, distinguished friends, and safe reputations, a world which had its iconography and managed to keep the important commissions in proper hands."[43] This could be said of most of the Commission of Fine Arts members.

Architects without the proper professional training had little chance of getting approval of their designs by the commission. Moore, as a layman, was not subject to charges of conflict of interest or favoritism to his own firm as were the artists and architects serving on the commission. He was freer, therefore, to practice professional elitism but certainly was not the only commission member who did so. James E. Fraser, a commissioner from 1920 to 1925 and noted sculptor who enjoyed many commissions in the capital, deplored awarding commissions to those whom he considered to be outsiders.

> A number of persons have recently come to Washington to secure commissions to paint portraits of public officials of the government; but whose work is not recognized by the leaders in the fine arts in this country, especially in painting and sculpture; that among these are foreigners who encroach upon the rights of American artists.[44]

The commission members were not merely college trained; they held their degrees from prestigious schools. Five of the original seven commission members held degrees from Harvard. (Burnham's Harvard degree was an honorary Master of Arts.) A study of the twenty-one architects who served be-tween 1910 and 1940[45] shows that at least twelve had attended Ivy League institutions (some do not list their undergraduate affiliations, so it could be higher); five had studied at Massachusetts Institute of Technology, and two-thirds of the twenty-one had continued their studies in Europe, most at the École des Beaux Arts in Paris.[46]

Architects serving on the commission tended to have apprenticed or worked at select architectural firms. Eight of the twenty-one had apprenticed at McKim, Mead, and White; William Adams Delano, who "was not conceived in the womb of McKim, Mead, and White,"[47] did the next best thing though: he apprenticed with Carrère and Hastings along with three other commission members. (Hastings himself apprenticed with McKim, Mead, and White.) The established Boston firm of Coolidge and Shattuck (later Shepley, Rutan, and Coolidge) also claimed three commission members; the Philadelphia firm of Zantzinger, Borie, and Medary two, both partners; and Burnham and Company, two—Burnham and Anderson.[48]

The twenty-one commissioners were active both in their local chapter and in the national organization of the American Institute of Architects. Four served as AIA national presidents and three as presidents of local chapters. Others were directors or chaired committees for the national or local organizations. Many combined work for the AIA with serving as a trustee for the American Academy in Rome or took an active role in the Society of Beaux Arts Architects in this country.[49]

All seven of the original commissioners were members of the Century Club, a New York City social club, "which for convenience during visits to studios of artists whose work was under consideration, became a sub-rosa annex to the Washington headquarters."[50] Of forty-five commissioners serving since 1910, forty of them were Century Club members and none came from west of the Mississippi.

> Whether this speaks well for our membership [the Century Club's], or is a form of nepotism, I hesitate to say. The answer probably is that, during the years since the Commission was established, it has never had a superabundance of funds, because Congress considers all commissions that deal with the fine arts as boutonnières on the lapels of really serious matters. Hence the difficulty of appointing men from the West, who would have had to make a long and expensive journey to Washington once a month.[51]

This homogeneity allowed an informality in the decision-making process that enhanced the closed-club character of the commission. Moore, following Burnham's example, did not run the monthly meetings in a formal fashion. The first meeting attended by only five of the commissioners on July 8, 1910, set the tone for the future, with the charmed circle of Charles Moore and his artist friends remaining remote from outsiders and their perhaps diverse ideas. As Moore recorded it:

> After a day of discussion, including a drive to those high spots Burnham ever sought to orient his mind with all outdoors, the chairman got down to real business; the welding of the members into a fellowship founded on the common loyalty to the ideals of President Washington as expressed in the plans of Major L'Enfant. Gathering his four companions around a table spread with his usual discriminating abundance, Burnham kept the talk loosely on capital problems, enlivened by Frank Millet's apt stories, Tommy Hastings's latest tricks, and Olmsted's

felicitously disputatious interpositions. One objective seen from a common point of view and discussed with entire openmindedness and tolerance: this ideal and practice the Commission ever maintained.[52]

The ability of the commission to remain a closed club over a period of thirty years was based on its success in controlling commission appointments.

All of the commission members appointed in 1910 had a four-year term. Taft, in appointing Blashfield and Anderson to replace Burnham and Millet in 1912, not only maintained the unanimity of viewpoint but the general composition of the commission made up of three architects, one landscape architect, one sculptor, one painter, and one layman.

In 1914, the members agreed among themselves and with President Woodrow Wilson to provide continuity of membership. Wilson agreed to appoint all the five remaining original members for another term with the stipulation that they arrange terms of service so that no more than two new members should be appointed each year.[53]

The sculptor Daniel Chester French either drew the short term or took it because he planned to resign anyway in 1915. Wilson asked the commission to recommend a successor. Herbert Adams, whom the commission had chosen to do the MacDonough Memorial in Plattsburg, New York, the year before, was chosen to replace French,[54] and Wilson made the appointment.

In 1916, Blashfield's and Anderson's terms expired—allowing the original four remaining members to stay on for another year. Wilson again followed commission recommendations and appointed architect Charles A. Platt and painter J. Alden Weir.[55]

In 1917, Hastings and Moore were to retire, and in 1918 Olmsted's and Gilbert's terms would expire. Gilbert, however, wanted to leave the commission for other reasons, so he and Moore changed places.[56] John Russell Pope was chosen by informal ballot to succeed Hastings; in the case of Gilbert, the discussion seemed to center on who from McKim, Mead, and White should replace him.[57] William Mitchell Kendall was eventually recommended, and Wilson again made the appointment. In 1918, Moore was unanimously recommended by his fellow commissioners for reappointment. In spite of Wilson's expressed desire that new persons be chosen, he made the appointment. Landscape architect James L. Greenleaf was chosen to replace Olmsted;[58] thus of the original members, only Moore remained.

To keep the commission intact, members were cautioned to exercise proper timing in announcing resignations. When artist William Sergeant Kendall notified the commission of his desire to resign before his term was up, he was asked to place his resignation in the hands of the commission to be delivered to the president—when the commission had already agreed on his successor. "Of course," the letter to Kendall continued, "your resignation should be addressed to the President."[59] The commission chose H. Siddons Mowbray, former director of the American Academy in Rome, as his successor.

Moore had direct access to the White House under Harding, Coolidge, and Hoover, so the commission had less to fear in regard to unfelicitous appointments. Moore, himself, continued to be recommended unanimously by his fellow commissioners for reappointment every four years.[60] As the public buildings program got under way in 1926, Moore asked that another person be appointed in his place. The commission's secretary, H. Paul Caemmerer, protested saying: "It is very important that Mr. Moore remain on the Commission since in all the great projects underway the Plan of 1901 is constantly referred to in connection with which he is constantly consulted, as also on Public Building matters."[61] Moore did remain on the commission for another fourteen years, and the commission members continued to hand pick their own successors throughout the years with Moore at the helm.

It was inevitable that commission members or their firms would want to compete for government projects and the issue of favoritism was bound to come up. The commissioners had voted as early as 1910 that there would be no objection to participation by its members in government competitions, but questions would be raised. Cass Gilbert, who asked the commission to rule on his eligibility for the Department of Justice Building competition, was especially concerned about the appearance of favoritism to himself or to one of the architects in his firm who had an entry in a monument competition that the commission had been asked to judge. He disqualified himself as a judge and asked that his action be so recorded.[62] Gilbert resigned from the commission in 1917, a year before his final design for the Treasury Annex came before the commission for its approval. Such niceties, however, made little difference, for the relationship between the present and past commissioners remained intimate. Moore, indeed, as noted earlier, encouraged past commissioners to remain in close contact, inviting them to attend meetings when subjects of special interest were to be discussed and including them in the social dinners that often followed meetings.

The commissioners recommended in 1914 that they not be asked to judge competitions; they felt they would risk alienating artists by declining such requests and suggested instead that a professional consultant be employed to engage an executive designer to take charge. The commission offered to furnish names of possible consultants.[63] Important commissions for public buildings and monuments in Washington, however, remained within a select group, a group increasingly dominated by Charles Moore. Commissioners such as John Russell Pope, Louis Ayres, Henry Bacon, William Mitchell Kendall, Charles Adams Platt, Cass Gilbert, Milton Medary, and William Adams Delano all were given important buildings to design in the capital, and the work of sculptor-commissioners James E. Fraser, Lorado Taft, Adolph Weinman, and Daniel Chester French is found throughout the city.

Shortly after Moore took over as chairman, the commission began to speak with one voice, but its ability to adhere to the 1901 plan without the aid of the sympathetic Taft was tested. Plans had been put forward by the government calling for a powerhouse to be built in Potomac Park. When, in 1916, William G. McAdoo, secretary of the Treasury, proved recalcitrant to consider alternate schemes, the Commission of Fine Arts, the Committee of 100,[64] and the American Federation of Art joined forces in a campaign to keep such unsightly smokestacks from Potomac Park. Charles Moore and Cass Gilbert, sitting in the Senate gallery during congressional debate on the issue, heard speakers single them out by name for derision.[65] When foundations at the proposed site proved unsatisfactory, the matter was dropped. While this cannot be called an actual victory for the commission, it apparently had its desired effect on

McAdoo and Wilson. Later when McAdoo offered Cass Gilbert the commission to design the Treasury Annex, Moore records that he told Gilbert: "President Wilson cautioned me not to run foul of the Commission of Fine Arts again."[66]

NOTES

1. John William Reps, *Monumental Washington: The Planning and Development of the Capital Center* (Princeton, N.J., 1967), 155.

2. Commission of Fine Arts. *Minutes*, May 18, 1911; November 25, 1911.

3. Ibid., July 14–15, 1911.

4. Charles Moore, *Daniel H. Burnham* (Boston, 1921), vol. 2: 152.

5. Charles Moore, *Memoirs*, 165. *Charles Moore Papers*, National Archives.

6. Commission of Fine Arts, *Ninth Annual Report*, July 1, 1919, to June 30, 1921 (Washington, D.C., 1921), 20.

7. Charles Moore and Glenn Brown were strong Republicans. McKim enjoyed the friendship of both Roosevelt and Taft, when Taft was secretary of war. Burnham and Moore were also friends of Taft's.

8. Glenn Brown, *Memories* (Washington, D.C., 1931), 195.

9. Moore, *Memoirs*, 167.

10. Harts served as ex-officio secretary of the commission from 1913 to 1917.

11. *Executive Order 1862*, November 28, 1913.

12. Commission of Fine Arts, *Annual Report*, 1914 (Washington, D.C., 1914), 14.

13. Ibid. L'Enfant did not extend the axis and place a memorial there. This was a common misconception.

14. Moore, *Memoirs*, 168–69.

15. H. Paul Caemmerer, "Charles Moore: Historian, Author, and City Planner." Unpublished manuscript in *Papers of Charles Moore*, RG 66, National Archives, 6.

16. Charles Moore to William Adams Delano, February 22, 1939. In *Papers of Charles Moore*, RG 66, National Archives, 2.

17. The group of architects who, under the aegis of the Treasury Department, were responsible for the design of the Federal Triangle.

18. Delano's essay appears in a commemorative volume, issued by the Century Association in celebration of its 100th anniversary. *The Century, 1847–1946* (New York, 1947), 222–23.

19. Charles Moore, "Personalities in Washington Architecture," *Columbia Historical Society Records* 37–38 (1937): 1–15.

20. Charles Moore, "Speech to the Washington Society of Fine Arts," February 18, 1937. Reprinted in the *Congressional Record* (March 1, 1937), 75th Cong. 1st sess., H.R. appendix, 372.

21. Quoted in Moore, "Personalities," 1.

22. Moore, "Speech," 373.

23. Charles Moore, "Standards of Taste," *American Magazine of Art* 21 (July 1930): 365.

24. Moore, "Personalities," 6.

25. Moore, *Memoirs*, 295.

26. See *Proceedings of the Thirty-fourth Annual Convention of the American Institute of Architects* (Washington, D.C., 1900); Glenn Brown, ed., *Improvement of the City of Washington, D.C.* (Washington, D.C., 1901); and Charles Moore, ed., *The Promise of American Architecture* (Washington, D.C., 1905).

27. Charles Moore, "The Government's Architectural Tradition," *Federal Architect* (January 1934): 8.

28. Moore, "Personalities," 3.

29. Charles Moore, "Washington as a Center of Culture," 1. Unpublished manuscript. In *General Correspondence*, RG 66, Records of the Commission of Fine Arts, National Archives.

30. Moore, "Personalities," 6.

31. Moore, "Washington as a Center of Culture," 2. Moore enjoyed repeating McKim's remark about the building, designed by A. B. Mullett in 1871–88, that he could help the building considerably if he had a rake ("Personalities," 7, and elsewhere). Moore gave support to Waddy B. Wood's scheme to remodel the building to be compatible with the Treasury.

32. Meigs had a plan for the Capitol.

33. Moore, "Washington as a Center of Culture," 2.

34. Moore, "Speech," 372.

35. Moore, "Standards of Taste," 365.

36. Charles Moore, "Washington—City of Splendor," *Current History* 2 (May 1930): 250.

37. Charles Moore, "Speech to Patriots and Pioneers Association, Kansas City." Reported in *Kansas City Times*, November 28, 1922. In *Charles Moore Papers*, RG 66, National Archives.

38. Charles Moore to William Adams Delano, November 22, 1939. In *Charles Moore Papers*, RG 66, National Archives.

39. Ibid.

40. Charles Moore, "The Transformation of Washington," *National Geographic* 4 (June 1923): 593.

41. Moore, *Memoirs*, 299–300. The meeting referred to was held March 15, 1928; the subject under discussion was the terminus of the axis running from the Capitol to the Lincoln Memorial. The 1901 plan proposed a watergate.

42. Ibid., 315.

43. Oliver W. Larkin, *Art and Life in America* (New York, 1949), 322.

44. Commission of Fine Arts. *Minutes*, March 21, 1917: 22–24.

45. The data were obtained from Henry F. Withey and Elsie Rathburn Withey, eds., *Biographical Dictionary of American Architects (Deceased)* (Los Angeles, 1970), and from the membership files of the American Institute of Architects.

46. Ivy Leaguers included Thomas Hastings, who served on the commission from 1910–17; Peirce Anderson, 1912–16; William Mitchell Kendall, 1916–21; Milton B. Medary, Jr., 1922–27; Benjamin W.

Morris, 1927–31; John W. Cross, 1928–33; Egerton Swartout, 1932–36; John Mead Howells, 1933–37; Charles A. Coolidge, 1933–36; Charles L. Borie, Jr., 1936–40; Henry R. Shepley, 1936–40; and William F. Lamb, 1937–45.

Kendall and Coolidge also studied at MIT along with Cass Gilbert, who served from 1910–16; Abram Garfield, 1925–30; and John L. Mauran, 1930–33.

Hastings, Anderson, Morris, Shepley, Cross, Howells, and Lamb, as well as John Russell Pope, who served from 1917–22, and William Adams Delano, 1924–28, all studied at the École des Beaux Arts. Gilbert, Kendall, Mauran, and Charles A. Platt, 1916–21, and Henry Bacon, 1921–24, all list study in Europe but do not specify where.

47. *The Century Association, 1847–1946* (New York, 1947), 205.

48. Hastings, Gilbert, Kendall, Bacon, Swartout, Garfield, and Howells, as well as Louis Ayres, who served from 1921–25, apprenticed at McKim, Mead, and White; Delano, Morris, and Lamb were with Carrère and Hastings; Coolidge, Shepley, and Mauran were at Coolidge and Shattuck and its successor; and Borie and Medary were from Zantzinger, Borie, and Medary.

49. Burnham, Gilbert, Medary, and Mauran were presidents of the national organization; Morris, Swartout, and Garfield were presidents of local chapters. Platt was president of the American Academy in Rome.

50. Moore, *Memoirs*, 156.

51. William Adams Delano quoted in *The Century*, 223. In discussing recommendations for new commissioners in 1925, the commissioners recorded in the *Minutes*: "It was thought that although there are good architects west of the Mississippi River, it would be too far for an architect to travel from that part of the country to attend commission meetings" (September 3, 1925).

52. Moore, *Memoirs*, 159. Olmsted, who was younger than the other Senate Park Commission members and responsible for drawing up the park system that stretched as far as Great Falls, possessed a broader view of planning and a greater sensitivity to the needs of the general public. Mel Scott in *American City Planning since 1890* (Berkeley, Calif., 1971) ex-

plores Olmsted's growing awareness of the need for planners to comprehend the complex web of the city in all its aspects and to intervene in the public interest where they could determine it. Olmsted, Jr., went to Harvard but did not seem to fit the philosophical mold of the other commissioners at the time.

53. Commission of Fine Arts. *Minutes*, May 7, 1917.

54. Ibid., November 25, 1914; May 20, 1915.

55. Ibid., July 14, 1916.

56. Ibid., May 7, 1917.

57. Ibid., May 7, 1917; July 14, 1916.

58. Ibid., July 26–27, 1918; September 4, 1918.

59. Maj. C. S. Ridley, commission secretary, to William Mitchell Kendall, November 16, 1920; Commission of Fine Arts. *Minutes*, November 13, 1920.

60. Commission of Fine Arts. *Minutes*, July 26–27, 1918; September 7, 1922; Commission Members to Herbert Hoover, [n.d.] 1930; Commission Members to Franklin D. Roosevelt, December 3, 1934. *Charles Moore Papers*, RG 66, National Archives.

61. Commission of Fine Arts. *Minutes*, December 2, 1926.

62. Ibid., November 2, 1911.

63. Commission of Fine Arts, *Annual Report*, 1914, 16.

64. The committee was formed in 1903 under the auspices of the American Civic Association to further the Senate Park Commission plan for Washington.

65. Moore, *Memoirs*, 170.

66. Ibid., 171.

CHAPTER III

PREPARING FOR THE PUBLIC BUILDINGS PROGRAM

1916–23

The Commission of Fine Arts was aware that the federal government's growing need for office space would mean a large-scale public buildings program. Its concern that any such program follow the 1901 plan and its desire to ensure a role for the private architect led the commission to seek a more aggressive role than its advisory position assigned by law. The unanimous dedication of the commission members to well-defined goals made them particularly effective in this more ambitious role, and the commission became the leader of the plan's supporters in the capital.

As early as 1911, the commission had approved the plans for three departmental buildings, the designs of which had been chosen in competitions sponsored under the stipulations of the Tarnsey Act. The proposed buildings were to be erected on a site the government had purchased running from Pennsylvania Avenue to B Street[1] between Fourteenth and Fifteenth streets, at the base of what later became known as the Federal Triangle. While the 1901 plan had called for an executive grouping around Lafayette Square facing the White House, it also allowed for public buildings along Fifteenth Street facing the White House lot. The buildings were to house the departments of State, Justice, and Labor and Commerce (Labor and Commerce were split into two departments in 1913). The Commission of Fine Arts was also pleased that Congress had made a start in purchasing the triangle area running from Sixth to Fifteenth streets between Pennsylvania Avenue and B Street, an important area that the Senate Park Commission had designated as the site of future public buildings. Changing administrations in 1912 and lack of congressional appropriations, however, prevented the construction of the three buildings. The need for office space continued to grow, and the high rental bill of the federal government was a large concern. The deterioration along Pennsylvania Avenue, a matter especially important to the Washington Board of Trade in 1901, had become worse.

In the spring of 1916, Moore and several commission members evaluated the role of the commission in a future building program. Commissioner Cass Gilbert wrote to Senator Francis O. Newlands of Nevada in April concerning the formation of a public buildings commission. Reporting on a conversation among Moore, Olmsted, Blashfield, and Col. William W. Harts, Gilbert told Newlands that they all realized the necessity for study and development of a complete plan for Washington and that it should be done by "those sympathetic to the L'Enfant Plan and the development of it made by the Burnham-McKim Commission." They had also discussed making the Commission of Fine Arts an executive body to act in this regard. While it had initially been agreed, Gilbert informed Newlands, that the commission should remain advisory, these members thought that it might be given "very limited powers of initiative in the sense of being authorized to suggest, from time to time, what line of development should be adopted and possibly be given a veto power to a very limited degree."[2]

Gilbert pointed out to Newlands that public buildings in recent years had not been erected under the Office of the Supervising Architect but rather under the office of Col. William Harts, officer-in-charge of Public Buildings and Grounds. Harts was sympathetic to the 1901 plan and a personal friend of President Wilson's, which made him an ideal executive officer of the Fine Arts Commission. Gilbert, however, expressed concern that they could not always be "assured of such an admirable officer as Colonel Harts" and that "the head of a new or special department [with responsibility for public buildings] might be a cubist, a futurist, or a Mullet [referring to A. B. Mullett, designer of the State, War, and Navy Building of 1871–88]." Gilbert recommended to Newlands that a special expert commission be appointed to prepare a plan subject to approval of the Commission of Fine Arts.[3]

Gilbert was more direct in his letter to Colonel Harts written the following day. He inquired "whether the whole work might not be entrusted to the Commission of Fine Arts." Once a general comprehensive plan had been prepared, it could be turned over to Harts's office, and the Commission of Fine Arts could return to its advisory role.[4]

Harts answered Gilbert that his proposal was "too ideal at this time."[5] How ideal was to be shortly demonstrated. The Public Buildings Commission proposed by Congress consisted of the chairman and a member of the Senate and House Committees on Appropriations and the Senate and House Committees on Public Buildings and Grounds, as well as Elliott Woods, superintendent of the Capitol, and James Wetmore, supervising architect of the Treasury.

It was not the type of expert commission Gilbert had in mind, and he wrote to Harts in May: "Better no commission than the one proposed." Gilbert found such a commission without vision, scholarship, or training. "Because a man is a Congressman, cabinet member or architect doesn't mean he is qualified."[6] Copies of the Gilbert and Harts correspondence had been sent to Moore. When the Public Buildings Commission as proposed was created later that year, Moore made an effort to have the 1901 models placed on display at the Capitol, feeling the new commission must be familiar with the 1901 plan before it began its work. In a letter to Arno B. Caemmerer, he pointed out that Architect of the Capitol Elliott Woods was "apt to be jealous and suspicious so the suggestion [for placing the models on display at the Capitol] must come from the Senate or House Committee on Public Buildings and Grounds."[7]

The legislation creating the Public Buildings Commission stipulated that the new commission should avail itself of the advice of the Commission of Fine Arts. Moore pointed this out to his commission in October of 1917 in a meeting where considerable time was devoted to discussing the arrangement of public buildings in Washington. Taking its role very seriously, the commission came to agreement that day on some important points: the Treasury Building, the Patent Office, the proposed State, Justice, and Commerce and Labor buildings, the Senate and House office buildings (designed by Carrère and Hastings) and the old Post Office on Seventh Street (now the Tariff Commission Building) were good and dignified types for departmental buildings, and the types of buildings appropriate for the Mall were the new National Museum (now National Museum of Natural History), the Department of Agriculture Building, the Freer Gallery, and the proposed George Washington Memorial Hall. It was also agreed that departmental buildings should be five stories and office buildings should be six or seven stories, the main consideration being good proportions. The commission continued to make a distinction between departmental buildings and office buildings, the latter requiring a simpler, less monumental treatment. The commission members

also now began to visit proposed building sites.[8]

No mention is made in the November *Minutes* of the proposed public buildings program, but at the December meeting, Moore laid before the commission a draft of a proposed letter to the Public Buildings Commission constituting its advice regarding the program.

The Public Buildings Commission had meanwhile been proceeding with a survey of the space presently owned and rented by the federal government and of its future requirements. Its goal was eventually to house all government activities in government-owned buildings in the city of Washington, and it prepared a list of possible future building sites. The Public Buildings Commission report was presented to Congress December 18, 1917,[9] and published in 1918. The published report included the Commission of Fine Arts report, but it had never been discussed or approved by the Public Buildings Commission or by Congress. Wartime pressures intervened and brought the matter to a halt. In January of 1918, however, Moore sent a copy of the recommendations made by the Commission of Fine Arts to various representatives asking, if they approved, to lend their aid in carrying them into execution. Moore's cover letter assured that "nothing more than good order and convenience in transacting business is aimed at."[10]

The advice of the Commission of Fine Arts, in reality a report of its own, began with a characteristic statement:

> This Commission therefore advises that the same ideas of good order and convenience which were the guiding principles in early days be followed in future buildings, and also that the precedents established by the chief struc-

tures of the earliest days determine the architectural styles for new buildings. The Commission has confidence in making this latter recommendation, because the style selected by the founders is the universal architectural language for the expression of ideas of permanency, dignity, and grandeur. Also because it is a style which permits variety in the treatment of individual buildings and which also is capable of expressing those varying degrees of subordination so essential to the harmonious arrangement of groups of buildings.[11]

The report recommended adhering to the 1901 plan by placing a legislative grouping around the Capitol and an executive grouping around the White House. Specifically, the sites between Fourteenth and Fifteenth streets were to be occupied by Justice, Commerce, and Labor (Commerce and Labor now being two separate departments). The State Department Building planned for the site in 1910 was to go to Lafayette Square. The character of the buildings on the Mall would be determined by those already there, or proposed for the area. Of the deterioration south of Pennsylvania Avenue in the Triangle, the report concluded that "nothing short of radical measures to bring this area into a higher grade of occupation will save the situation." It urged the government to acquire the land for future public buildings, including an archives building, and pointed out the advantages of centralizing government activities in terms of efficiency and convenience.[12] Despite its lack of official approval, the report would prove a solid base on which to build after the war.

As the war became imminent, Moore moved his residence to Washington and accepted the post as acting chief of the manuscript division of the Library of Congress. He was then chosen to accompany Arthur C. McLaughlin,[13] who was president of the American Historical Association (AHA), to England to interpret the spirit of the United States. Moore, who had received a Ph.D. in history from George Washington University in 1900, served as the treasurer of the AHA. In 1918, at the age of sixty-three, Moore was reappointed by President Wilson as chairman of the Commission of Fine Arts.

The commission remained active during the war, concerning itself with designs for medals and discharge certificates, as well as follow-up work on building projects already under way. Toward the end of the war, the commission worked on the designs for military cemeteries and gravestones, and it also prepared a report on appropriate war memorials, listing a person to be contacted in each state for advice on selecting an artist.[14] In spite of the war, the number of submissions disposed of annually by the commission continued to rise each year.

Moore was particularly active in opposing the erection of temporary buildings on the Mall during the war. He also made a trip to Europe with a special commission to select sites for American cemeteries.[15]

When the war ended, the commission and Moore were quick to return to their major concerns as the country adjusted to peacetime. The *Annual Report* of 1919 contains a section entitled, "The Future Development of Washington," which is introduced by the assertion: "Probably the next quarter of a century will mark the greatest building activity ever undertaken by the Government since the City of Washington was begun. . . . New buildings . . . should not be set down in haphazard fashion." The report called for the purchase of the area between the Capitol and the Treasury bounded by Pennsylvania Avenue, Fourteenth and B streets (the government already owned the base of the Triangle between Fourteenth and

Fifteenth streets) and for the construction of public buildings including Justice, Commerce, Labor, Archives, a municipal market, an armory, and exhibition and convention halls.[16]

The report summarized the needs to be met in the future: the removal of temporary buildings from the Mall and Potomac Park, completion of the central composition from the Capitol to the Lincoln Memorial, completion of the Anacostia Water Park, the purchase of Mount Hamilton for the National Botanical Gardens, and completion of parkway connections. It also called for zoning for the District and the establishment of garden suburbs, a reflection of the growing national interest in urban planning.[17]

Moore was particularly anxious to keep the 1901 plan in the public eye as proposals for future buildings were discussed. His work during these years before the Public Buildings Act was passed by Congress in 1926 was extremely important in formulating public opinion and influencing decision makers and thus in determining official guidelines. The 1921 *Annual Report* contained a chapter on the history, progress, present status, and future realization of the McMillan Plan. It was reprinted by the commission and made available to the public at twenty cents.[18] In 1922, Moore arranged to have the 1901 models put on display at the National Museum so the public could see them, and at the July meeting the commission members themselves went to the museum to view the models.

As pressure mounted throughout 1922 for a public buildings bill in Congress, Moore faced two battles encountering bitter opposition but emerged not only victorious but with his own position considerably enhanced. The first involved the design and location of the Arlington Memorial Bridge.

The building of a memorial bridge across the Potomac had been the subject of a number of studies. A competition had been sponsored by the government in 1900 to select a design for a bridge located on a line with New York Avenue at 23d Street. The firm of Burr and Casey had won the competition with a design for a high, elaborately monumental bridge. The Senate Park Commission in extending the central axis to the site for the Lincoln Memorial had located the bridge at its terminus on a line with the Custis-Lee Mansion in Arlington Cemetery across the river. McKim's conception of the bridge, shown in the pictorial renderings that accompanied the report, was of a low bridge with simple, classical lines.

The Arlington Memorial Bridge Commission was created in 1913, but no money for construction was appropriated. After the war, the Commission of Fine Arts pushed for construction of the bridge. In 1922, Col. Clarence O. Sherrill, officer-in-charge of public buildings and grounds, recommended the location on a line with New York Avenue to the Memorial Commission headed by President Harding. The Commission of Fine Arts issued a report protesting the choice of location and advocated the site assigned the bridge by the Senate Park Commission. The collective report was supplemented by individual reports by the commission members.[19] At this point, Moore decided on a bold move. Fearing the reports would be pigeonholed, he released them to the press, which brought him a rebuke by letter from President Harding.[20] In apologizing, Moore questioned whether Harding thought the opinions of the Commission of Fine Arts should be withheld from the press. Harding answered again by saying it was "only proper to go to the Commission first" as a "courtesy."[21] Nevertheless, Harding called a special meeting of the Memorial Commission to reconsider the matter, and it decided in favor of the location chosen by the Senate Park Commission by the Lincoln Memorial.[22] According to Moore's *Memoirs*, Grace Coolidge told Moore that when her husband, the vice president, returned from this meeting of the Memorial Bridge Commission, he told her that "Mr. Moore won on the bridge matter." Mrs. Coolidge asked, "Did you help him?" "No. He didn't need it," returned the vice president.[23]

The Commission of Fine Arts was then asked to name three architects to design the bridge. It suggested the firm of McKim, Mead, and White, and Charles A. Platt, and Paul Cret.[24] Colonel Sherrill chose McKim, Mead, and White, which meant that William Mitchell Kendall, a Fine Arts Commission member from 1916 to 1921 and McKim's assistant up to the time of his death, would do the design.

Moore's maneuver was especially risky in light of the fact that he had recently been under attack in Congress for his efforts to implement a proposal for Union Square at the head of the Mall where the botanical gardens were located. The 1901 plan had suggested a national arboretum be built on Mount Hamilton to replace the antiquated gardens. The Grant Monument was already being constructed on part of the gardens, which also furnished flowers and shrubs to congressmen and thus had a certain amount of popularity among the legislators. Moore had been seeking national support for the proposed arboretum on Mount Hamilton from garden clubs and botanical societies throughout the nation. The superintendent of the gardens had influential friends in Congress who joined with him to fight against the removal of the gardens. One of them, Representative William Wood, deliv-

ered a speech in the House vehemently attacking Moore, saying at one point that he was "nothing but a toad."[25] Wood, who was the head of the subcommittee that considered the commission's appropriations, then continued his grievance against Moore in a letter to President Harding in which he charged that Moore had been reimbursed for nonallowable expenses and protested his reappointment. Moore successfully defended himself in a letter to Harding[26] and was unanimously recommended by his fellow commissioners for reappointment.[27] Harding made the appointment. Moore was proving remarkably durable.

Moore was now free to turn his attention to the debate over a public buildings program that was going on in Congress. The Public Buildings Commission under the leadership of Senator Reed Smoot prepared another report that was presented to Congress on January 5, 1923. Even before the report was completed, the newspapers were agitating for a buildings program. The *Washington Star* was active in pointing out the cost and inefficiency of the scattering of departments and bureaus in rented office space throughout the District, noting that the Internal Revenue Service was in eight different locations and the Department of Agriculture in twenty-two.[28]

Those in Congress who opposed an immediate buildings program argued that the housing crisis should be solved first, that such a program should be instituted when the nation was undergoing an economic slump rather than in a period of prosperity, and such a program had pork-barrel features. Those who favored a buildings program pointed to increased efficiency and lower costs of housing the activities of government in government-owned buildings and, in the case of the proposed archives, to the danger to improperly housed records from fire and water.[29]

In February, Representative John W. Langley, who headed the House Committee on Public Buildings and Grounds, announced that he would push for a general public buildings program that would include an acropolis at Massachusetts Avenue and W Street containing a conservatory of music and a temple of tribute to motherhood. Shortly afterward, Langley met with Moore, and no mention again appears of the suggested acropolis at a location outside the center of Washington.[30] Langley's next statement in April, as he was about to introduce a public buildings bill in the House, shows he had done a complete turnabout. Langley stressed the efficiency and economy of constructing the necessary buildings and stated:

> They should, of course, harmonize with the general plans for the Arlington Memorial Bridge and the other structures already completed or in contemplation which are in keeping with the general program of the Fine Arts Commission and other experts and with what seems to be practically the unanimous sentiment of Congress.[31]

Moore's success in modifying Langley's views was not unusual. He was persuasive and adept at stressing those aspects of a program that Congress publicly loved to espouse, such as efficiency and economy. He was equally skillful in convincing legislators that public sentiment favored the 1901 plan and its various facets.

Moore was eager to have the legislation passed but put his efforts into securing a role for the commission in the proposed buildings program. He received support from President Harding and his cabinet who were unanimously in favor of the building and development plan of the Commission of Fine

Arts that "would transfer the south side of Pennsylvania Avenue into a great park, dotted here and there with magnificent buildings."[32] Moore continued to differentiate, however, between departmental and office buildings throughout his work on the Federal Triangle. It was a useful stratagem for reassuring those who felt that monumentality was a waste of the taxpayers' money. As a precept, it fitted Moore's ideas of appropriateness and suitability.

Moore told Milton Medary, a Philadelphia architect, who in June 1923 was heading the AIA's Committee on Public Works and serving on the Commission of Fine Arts, that he also advised Harding himself to keep command of the Federal Triangle project. He pointed out to him that "Senator Smoot's chief idea was economy and the saving of rents paid to private owners of buildings, whereas Mr. Langley . . . was looking out primarily for country post offices and was willing to provide for the national government in Washington incidentally; also that if there is not an orderly arrangement for building, the most urgent needs will be subordinated and the person who has favor with Congress will get his building ahead of those more needed."[33]

Moore suggested to Medary that his committee of the AIA "discuss quite seriously the relation of the architectural profession to the building problem in Washington." Moore said he thought the committee should meet with the Commission of Fine Arts and "together we should consider the matter of the location of departmental and other buildings, the methods of selecting architects, the government official who shall act as professional adviser, the necessity for adequate consideration of the various projects, the subordination of one project to another, and other like matters."[34]

No bill, however, was passed by Congress at that time, and, in August, President Harding died. Moore had assiduously cultivated both President and Mrs. Harding, basking again in the favor of a Republican president. He had, early in the Harding administration, sent Mrs. Harding books and pictures on the history and traditions of the White House, and he was frequently invited to social functions there.[35] The relationship, however, remained quite formal. Moore's relationship with Calvin Coolidge as president, on the contrary, had become extremely friendly.

Moore had met the Coolidges through common friends when Coolidge was governor of Massachusetts. When Coolidge was elected vice president and he and his wife moved to Washington, they found the congenial Moore, who was so knowledgeable about the capital, a welcome companion. Moore invited the vice president and Mrs. Coolidge to be the guests of the commission for luncheon the day the commission members viewed the 1901 models at the National Museum,[36] and he arranged a special slide show in conjunction with the Committee of 100.[37]

Letters to Moore from Grace Coolidge reveal that they were close and intimate friends. She often addressed her letters to him as "Dear Sir Knight" or "Dear Sir Knight of the Arts," and signed them "Your Princess." Moore was in Europe when Harding died on August 2, 1923. Grace Coolidge, writing him on black-edged stationery less than two weeks later, opined: "I cannot say anything you do not know and understand."[38]

During the six years that Coolidge was president, Moore had regularly scheduled monthly meetings with Mrs. Coolidge and received many invitations to the White House for both formal and informal occasions. In his *Memoirs*, Moore recounts a conversation he and Grace Coolidge arranged ahead of time to acquaint the president with a problem regarding the botanical gardens and its superintendent who was planning to build new greenhouses.[39] The rehearsed dialogue was performed in the private dining room of the White House. Moore wrote of it: "This conversation was simply for the President's benefit—to make him acquainted with a very pressing problem with which she herself had been made well acquainted."[40]

Moore as well as the Commission of Fine Arts as an institution was enjoying increasing prestige at this time. "The Commission boldly proclaims the purpose 'to create on the banks of the Potomac a unified, organized and magnificent capital city to express by its permanence and grandeur the power and stability of the Republic.'"[41]

Moore's burgeoning influence and the commission's growing prestige were especially important at this time when guidelines were being drawn for the long-delayed great public buildings program. Increasingly, the commission took the position of leadership among those organizations that had been allied with it in the battle to assure that Washington developed according to the plan of 1901. At the same time, some of the commission's allies were either weakened or distracted.

The Committee of 100 had worked assiduously to defend the 1901 plan since its inception in 1903. The committee had benefited from the leadership of such knowledgeable and dedicated Washingtonians as Glenn Brown. In the 1920s, however, its members became increasingly concerned by the failure of the government to acquire parkland and to plan comprehensively for the entire region. As a result, the committee began to work for the establishment of a park and planning commission for the District of Columbia. The District had adopted zoning laws and set up a zoning commission in 1920. As early as 1910, legislation had been enacted limiting the height of the buildings to the width of the street plus twenty feet, with a maximum of 130 feet. This did not include federal buildings, however, and the commission carefully monitored building height, ensuring the growth of Washington as a horizontal city. While features of the plan of 1901—especially those relating to the central composition—had been realized, the acquisition of parkland had not kept pace with population growth.[42] There was no planning agency to concern itself with the regional character of the capital, with its setting, its housing, traffic, transportation, playgrounds, and schools. Even if the leadership of the Commission of Fine Arts had desired to deal with some of these growing problems, broad changes in the power and organization of the commission would have been necessary to allow it to deal effectively with them. Moore's interests went far beyond monumental Washington, but his concern with schools, bridges, hospitals, parks, parkways, and entrances into the city was almost totally aesthetic. Thus when Olmsted and the Committee of 100 turned their interest in civic improvement to broader planning concepts, the more narrowly perceived, mainly aesthetic goals of the Commission of Fine Arts no longer had the benefit of their total effort. In 1924, the National Capital Park Commission was established, which evolved in 1926 into the National Capital Park and Planning Commission.[43]

The American Institute of Architects had been another strong ally, continuing in the 1920s to work closely with the commission.

Like the Committee of 100, however, it too organized in support of a planning commission, forming the Committee on the Plan of Washington and Environs; a member in each chapter of the institute was designated to keep local membership informed on the authorization of a city-planning commission for the capital.[44] The AIA did not approach the development of Washington with the single-mindedness of the Commission of Fine Arts, nor did it have the commission's prestige. Henry Saylor in his history of the AIA points out its relatively low status at this time:

> Back in the days of supermen like Burnham and McKim, the Institute's voice had commanded attention, but there had followed a long period in which the Institute was, to official Washington, just another trade group.[45]

The institute had lost the leadership of Glenn Brown in 1913 when a major reorganization distributing power among the various chapters brought about his resignation. Brown's loyalty to the 1901 plan and its creators, especially McKim, was very great indeed, and he had been able to mobilize the institute in its defense whenever necessary.

The commission as much as the AIA, and at times more effectively, continued to battle for private architects attempting to gain government commissions, negotiate contracts, establish fees, work within government regulations, and win recognition from the federal government. The Tarnsey Act had been repealed in 1912 because the government objected to paying the usual fees charged by private architects. Moore was acutely aware of this problem.

In an article written for the AIA's journal entitled, "The Government and the Practicing Architect," Moore pointed out that while relations between the government and the practicing architect had been a subject of discussion for years, no basis of agreement had been found to govern the relationship. The Tarnsey Act itself had not always been enforced.

> The present practice of leaving the architects employed on government work to make their own bargains with officials in charge of building has led to uncertainty, lack of uniformity and frequent differences of opinion, which not infrequently have resulted in changes in architects. The point of view of the official and the architect results from misunderstandings on both sides. [46]

Fee bargaining remained a major problem. William Adams Delano found out that the self-assured Cass Gilbert had gotten a much higher fee for doing the Supreme Court Building than he had been offered for the Post Office and it gave him a "decided inferiority complex." [47] Burt L. Fenner of McKim, Mead, and White came to Moore to ask advice on the fee for Arlington Memorial Bridge. In his *Memoirs*, Moore wrote:

> I, knowing well various grievous upsets of the architects over that vexed question, said to him: "McKim, Mead and White want to design that bridge. Don't get into a dispute over fees. State your office costs and stipulate for enough to cover them. Beyond that take what you two parties can amicably agree upon. The Government balks at paying fees set for private work however just." [48]

Low commissions, uncollected fees, and the problems related to understanding and meeting government specifications continued to plague the private architects in dealing with the government. Moore and the commission proved much more effective in helping the architects obtain government commissions and in guarding their designs against unfortunate changes by government officials than they did in regulation of fees. The assistance of the commission went only to established architects and their firms, whose work could be counted on to be in the classical tradition for important public buildings.

The AIA did attempt some aggressive action aimed at increasing its control over the development of Washington. In 1921, the Washington chapter organized an advisory council to render voluntary service in passing on all plans filed for private building permits. This attempt to do for the private sector what the commission was doing for the public sector had no legality and was completely dependent on the willingness of private builders to submit their plans to the council. The AIA's Committee on Public Works under the leadership of Milton Medary and William Adams Delano was active in seeking to increase the role of the private architect in the design of public buildings and cooperated closely with the Commission of Fine Arts, but the initiative in the period before the public buildings program got under way remained in the hands of the commission.

NOTES

1. B Street became Constitution Avenue in February 1931.

2. Cass Gilbert to Francis O. Newlands, April 13, 1916. *Project Files*, RG 66, National Archives.

3. Ibid.

4. Gilbert to William W. Harts, April 14, 1916. *Project Files*, RG 66, National Archives.

5. Harts to Gilbert, April 18, 1916. *Project Files*, RG 66, National Archives.

6. Gilbert to Harts, May 5, 1916. *Project Files*, RG 66, National Archives.

7. Moore to Arno B. Caemmerer, December 18, 1916. *Project Files*, RG 66, National Archives. Harts served as executive officer to the Public Buildings Commission and Arno Caemmerer as secretary.

8. Commission of Fine Arts. *Minutes*, October 13, 1917; October 27, 1917.

9. *S.D. 155*, 65th Cong. 2d Sess.

10. Moore to Congressional Representatives, January [n.d.] 1918. *Project Files*, RG 66, National Archives.

11. The entire report of the Commission of Fine Arts to the Public Buildings Commission was reprinted as part of the Commission of Fine Arts' *Annual Report, 1916–1918*, 8–32.

12. Ibid., 15.

13. Constance McLaughlin Green's father.

14. Commission of Fine Arts. *Minutes*, October 17, 1919; idem, *Annual Report, 1919* (Washington, D.C., 1920), 27–52.

15. Moore took the trip in the autumn of 1919, accompanied by William Mitchell Kendall and James Greenleaf. A copy of their report is among the *Charles Moore Papers*, RG 66, National Archives.

16. Commission of Fine Arts, *Annual Report, 1919*.

17. Ibid., 18–20.

18. Commission of Fine Arts. *Minutes*, November 1911; December 1921.

19. Ibid., September 7, 1922.

20. President Harding to Moore, September 25, 1922. *Charles Moore Papers*, Box 10, Library of Congress.

21. Harding to Moore, October 6, 1922. *Charles Moore Papers*, Box 10, Library of Congress.

22. Joanna Zangrando, *Monumental Bridge Design in Washington, D.C., as a Reflection of American Culture, 1886 to 1932*, Ph.D. Dissertation (George Washington University, 1974), gives a full account of Moore's role in determining location and design of the bridge.

23. Charles Moore, *Memoirs*, 298. *Records of the Commission of Fine Arts*, RG 66, Charles Moore Papers, National Archives.

24. Zangrando, *Monumental Bridge Design*, 369.

25. Moore, *Memoirs*, 301.

26. Moore to Harding, [August 1922?]. *Charles Moore Papers*, Box 10, Library of Congress.

27. Commission of Fine Arts. *Minutes*, September 7, 1922.

28. *Washington Star*, December 29, 1922; February 13, 1923.

29. *Washington Post*, January 8, 1923; January 15, 1923; *Washington Star*, February 1, 1923; April 14, 1923; April 22, 1923; August 17, 1923; August 23, 1923.

30. *Washington Star*, February 19, 1923.

31. *Washington Star*, April 22, 1923.

32. *Washington Post*, January 1, 1923.

33. Moore to Milton B. Medary, Jr., June 2, 1923. *Project Files*, RG 66, National Archives.

34. Ibid.

35. Harding Correspondence. *Charles Moore Papers*, Box 10, Library of Congress.

36. Commission of Fine Arts. *Minutes*, July 20, 1922.

37. Charles Moore, "Speech to the Washington Society of Fine Arts," February 18, 1937. Reprinted in *Congressional Record* (March 1, 1937), 75th Cong. 1st Sess. H.R. appendix, 371–73.

38. Grace Coolidge to Moore, October 3, 1922;

November 23, 1922; August 15, 1923. *Charles Moore Papers*, Box 10, Library of Congress.

39. Olmsted, Jr., led the fight, which was finally won in 1937, for the removal of the botanical gardens from the head of the Mall with Moore's full support.

40. Moore, *Memoirs*, 310.

41. *New York Times*, "Control of Civic Art" (editorial), November 16, 1925.

42. U. S. Grant III quoted the following statistics: From 1901 to 1925, parkland in the District increased 24 percent while population increased 70 percent. "The L'Enfant Plan and Its Evolution," *Columbia Historical Society Records* 33–34 (1932): 16.

43. Olmsted, Jr., was appointed to the new commission, along with Frederic A. Delano, J. C. Nichols of Kansas City, Missouri, and Milton Medary. Maj. U. S. Grant III, director of Public Buildings and Parks, was named executive and disbursing officer.

44. Harold W. Peaslee, "The Federal City Planning Commission," *American City* 33 (August 1925): 188. Peaslee, who was chairman of the AIA Committee on the Plan of Washington and Its Environs, also had an article on its efforts to obtain a planning commission on the front page of the editorial section of the *Washington Star*, January 25, 1925.

45. Henry Saylor, *The AIA's First Hundred Years, 1857–1957* (Washington, D.C., 1957), 47.

46. Charles Moore, "The Government and the Practicing Architect," *Journal of the American Institute of Architects* 16 (March 1928): 90. The heart of the article is an exchange of letters between Superintendent of the Library of Congress Bernard R. Green and Charles McKim that took place in 1904. Green stressed the need of the government to manage all its own enterprises, and McKim argued for architects to supervise the ongoing work on structures they design.

47. William Adams Delano, "Memoirs of Centurion Architects," in *The Century, 1847–1946* (New York, 1947), 209.

48. Moore, *Memoirs*, 299.

CHAPTER IV

A MANDATE
FOR GRANDEUR

1923–29

Iit was increasingly evident that action on a public buildings program could not be far off. In August 1923, less than a week after Coolidge took office, Lt. Col. Clarence O. Sherrill announced that there was no more office space to be found in the District.[1] In September, shortly after the Coolidges were installed in the White House living quarters, Moore and President Coolidge's physician, Brig. Gen. Charles E. Sawyer, an active member of the Committee of 100, were dinner guests in the family dining room. Moore recorded a conversation between himself and the president: "If the Commission of Fine Arts had the money," Coolidge asked, "could you build the buildings the Government needs?"

"Yes," Moore replied, "if it came slowly enough." Moore went on to explain that a large lump appropriation involved waste and graft whereas a "continuing appropriation of five or ten million a year would permit five or ten buildings to be kept going efficiently and economically."[2] In October, Coolidge took the matter up with his cabinet, and the *Washington Star* reported that Coolidge was convinced that the housing for government departments was urgent but that "rather than a huge general building bill the president would insist upon starting with a plan for the erection of five or six governmental buildings." He would specify, reported the *Star*, neither particular buildings nor particular sites, but "was represented as favoring the plan drawn up by the arts commission and was willing to leave it to the discretion of this body to carry it out." The president wanted buildings "magnificent in architecture and general in aspect . . . in harmony with the general run of our public buildings."[3] At the March 1924 meeting of the commission, Moore reported that his advice on the public buildings program had been sought by government officials in accordance with the president's request. Moore's answer had been to refer the officials to the *Public Buildings Report* of 1917 based on the 1901 plan and approved by the Commission of Fine Arts.[4]

Coolidge's desire for a limited building program was opposed by Representative Langley who intimated that it was all or nothing.[5] For the next two years, debate over the so-called pork-barrel features of the proposed general public buildings bill would hold up the legislation. Early in 1925, President Coolidge made public a fifty-million-dollar public buildings program for the District of Columbia[6]—in keeping with the limited program he had discussed with Moore, which Moore and the Commission of Fine Arts continued to favor.[7] It appeared, however, that the District buildings program could not pass Congress unless tied to a bill that would provide new buildings throughout the country.[8]

The Public Buildings Commission[9] under Senator Reed Smoot continued to advocate a public buildings bill. In January 1926, the Senate Committee on Public Buildings and Grounds, chaired by Senator Smoot, reported favorably on an omnibus bill that allowed $50 million for the District, $100 million for buildings throughout the country, and $15 million to complete the unfinished portion of the 1913 Public Buildings Program. Control of the program continued to be an issue, with opposition in Congress to placing control in the executive branch.[10]

The disgraceful conditions along Pennsylvania Avenue were a stimulus to congressional approval. The ceremonial avenue was lined with gas stations, tattoo parlors, chop suey signs, rooming houses, and cheap hotels.[11] Ohio Avenue, which cut through the Triangle, was lined with brothels. Moore credited a desire on the part of Congress to

do something about these conditions with aiding the eventual passage of the Public Buildings Act in 1926.[12] Maj. U. S. Grant III, who replaced Colonel Sherrill as director of Public Buildings and Public Parks for the District[13] in 1926, would later comment that the public buildings program was "our first great urban development and slum clearance project."[14]

Congressional concern with conditions in the Triangle was effectively exploited by the supporters of the Public Buildings Act by stipulating that the proposed new buildings should be located there. This was accomplished by the Bruce amendment that provided that none of the money appropriated should be expended on any sites for new buildings north of Pennsylvania or New York avenues. The *Washington Post* applauded the concentration of the new buildings between the White House and the Capitol, saying it would make "a real government community."[15] Senator William Cabell Bruce, the author of the amendment, made use of the rhetoric so often employed by the defenders of the 1901 plan by saying: "The amendment I have offered contemplates nothing less than a return to the original plan designed by L'Enfant and supervised by Washington and Jefferson for the development of the City of Washington." Bruce also argued that his plan had the support of the press and "approval of more than one architect of distinction."[16]

The Public Buildings Act with the Bruce amendment passed both houses and was signed by President Coolidge on May 25, 1926. The pork-barrel debate had been resolved by giving the Public Buildings Commission authority over what buildings were to be built, and their cost and location. Design and construction would come under Andrew Mellon,[17] secretary of the treasury.

While both the conditions along Pennsylvania Avenue and the acute need for office space played a large part in the passage of the bill, statements by both Secretary Mellon and Senator Smoot at this time demonstrated that they too had been caught up in Moore's cause.

> As one proceeds down Pennsylvania Avenue toward the Capitol on the south side will be a succession of beautiful and harmonious buildings, all of a design in keeping with the semi-classical tradition so well established in Washington.[18]

While Mellon apparently had no need to be convinced that the new departmental buildings should be monumental and not merely utilitarian, the economically minded Senator Smoot had apparently yielded to the excitement of the day. The new buildings, he said, "are to be architecturally beautiful as well as adequate in size and practical for the use to which they are to be put . . . monuments for all times and which Congress and the [Public Buildings] commission want to compare favorably with the finest offered by the capitals of the world."[19]

Others began to advocate the proposed building program; Otto Wilson called it a "realization of a dream of civic beauty . . . making Washington the queen of all the cities in the world."[20] It must have sounded agreeable to Charles Moore who had worked assiduously with other members of the commission to create just that sort of climate. With the passage of the bill, location and design, however, began to draw Moore's attention, and the two commissions met for a joint meeting. At the meeting,

> Mr. [Milton] Medary urged the importance of preparing a plan for public buildings to cover the entire area south of Pennsylvania Avenue

and west of Maryland Avenue, and called attention to the Chicago World's Fair where the buildings were properly related to each other. Similarly, he said, the L'Enfant Plan provides for a group of buildings in this space under consideration, and they should be so placed and related to each other as to give the idea of grandeur of the composition.[21]

Rather than attempting to spend $10 million a year on the proposed buildings, Medary also suggested that the government purchase the land needed for the new buildings before prices would increase. Agitation had begun for purchase of the entire Triangle by the federal government before the Public Buildings Act. It had been proposed in 1925, and at that time, the *Washington Post* had pointed out that it had been recommended as a "logical area of development" by the Senate Park Commission and that Congress should not delay in taking action.[22] The Bruce amendment had made such a purchase a virtual necessity. Toward the end of 1926, the press took up the cause. A *Washington Star* editorial urged that the government "take the whole Triangle now."[23] The *Post* pointed out that Mellon supported immediate purchase and that a proposal for its purchase would have support from Coolidge, the Commission of Fine Arts, and the newly formed National Capital Park and Planning Commission.[24] Mellon pointed out, reported the *Star*, the obvious economical advantage of buying the entire area at once rather than acquiring it piecemeal and allowing speculators to bargain and drive up the prices.[25] The *Washington Herald* called buying the land a "twenty-five year old McMillan project."[26]

Milton Medary wrote to Moore in September: "It is very interesting to see the trend toward our original recommendation that the first monies should be spent in securing land within the Triangle."[27] The Public Buildings Commission and Mellon had already assured Moore that the immediate purchase of the Triangle would be recommended to Congress.[28] While it took over a year to get the necessary legislation through Congress, on January 13, 1928, legislation was passed authorizing acquisition of all private lands in the Triangle. This assured a concentration of government buildings between the White House and the Capitol and made possible a design of a single general scheme for the total area.

The two commissions also assigned locations for proposed public buildings based on the Commission of Fine Arts' recommendations of 1917. The Justice, Commerce, and Labor Department buildings were to be on the Fifteenth Street sites extending from Pennsylvania Avenue to B Street, and the Archives Building between Twelfth and Thirteenth streets. It was also agreed at the meeting that the Internal Revenue Service Building should be erected south of the Post Office Building between Tenth and Eleventh streets on a square presently owned by the government and that the central portion of the Department of Agriculture should be completed.[29]

The Commission of Fine Arts advocated that the necessary government buildings be erected in the Triangle not only because both the L'Enfant plan and the 1901 plan placed public buildings there, but because they were committed to protecting the park-like quality of the Mall. The commission also wanted the buildings facing directly on the Mall limited to those with public access, such as museums. The Department of Agriculture Building had been located there before the creation of the commission in 1910, but the commission wanted no more office buildings on the Mall.[30]

The department secretaries, however, had their own views on the matter. Secretary of Commerce Herbert Hoover wanted the Commerce Building on the Mall, and the Public Buildings Commission tentatively placed it on the Mall between Twelfth and Fourteenth streets opposite the Department of Agriculture Building to appease him. The commission opposed it,[31] as did Secretary of Agriculture W. M. Jardine, who wanted that area, then the site of the department's greenhouses, reserved for the Department of Agriculture's expansion.[32] The Public Buildings Commission referred the matter for consideration to the Commission of Fine Arts.[33]

Moore and the Commission of Fine Arts wanted neither of the buildings on the Mall. Moore met with representatives from the Department of Agriculture, and it became apparent the department was more interested in preserving the Mall area where their greenhouses were located than in further expansion there.[34] Jardine continued to oppose a Mall location for Commerce, but made no further mention of Agriculture expanding there, a position that proved very helpful to the commission. Jardine supported the commission's attempt to relocate the markets administered by the Department of Agriculture in the Triangle.[35] Moore also managed to convince Commerce to take the Fifteenth Street site facing the White House.[36]

At its meeting on September 16, the commission reaffirmed that no departmental office building should be erected on the Mall and that Commerce should be located on an enlarged site between Fourteenth and Fifteenth streets. Justice was moved to a site between Fourth and Sixth streets.[37] The Public Buildings Commission announced, two days later, that it would stand firm on a Mall location for Commerce.[38] At a special meeting held September 21, however, attended by Secretary Mellon and Assistant Secretary of the Treasury Charles Dewey,[39] Secretary Hoover and Assistant Secretary of Commerce Drake, several members of the Public Buildings Commission[40] and Moore, the Commerce Building was successfully relocated to Pennsylvania Avenue between Fourteenth and Fifteenth streets.[41]

The commission's stand on the Mall was supported by the Washington papers. The *Post* said public opinion was against any encroachment on the Mall, and the people were grateful to the Commission of Fine Arts for protecting it.[42]

With every reason to feel its decision would prevail, the commission on the eve of its October meeting released the text of a letter written to Senator Smoot, as chairman of the Public Buildings Commission, to the newspapers. The letter, published in the *Washington Star* on October 12, 1926, recommended that the Mall be reserved for museum buildings that could be restricted to a height uniform with other buildings on the Mall and that could include landscaping essential to park buildings. This would preclude its use by the departments of Agriculture or Commerce. The letter suggested that the Department of Commerce Building be located instead on Fifteenth Street from Pennsylvania Avenue to B Street.

The enlarged Pennsylvania Avenue site allotted for the Commerce Building between Fifteenth and Fourteenth streets between Constitution and Pennsylvania avenues stemmed directly from Hoover's insistence on a building large enough to house all the department's activities under one roof. But Mellon opposed the idea of a building of such great size in the District of Columbia,[43] and the commission suggested instead that bureaus in the department be located in separate buildings in the area and connected by arcades and underground passageways.[44] Moore discussed the matter with Philip Sawyer of York and Sawyer, whose firm had won the competition for the design of the Commerce and Labor Building in 1910 and who expected to design the proposed Commerce Building as well. Sawyer agreed that the building should be limited in size and told Moore "he would fight it out along those lines although it meant less of a job."[45]

Hoover, however, who had been talked out of a Mall site, was adamant on the larger building. The suitability of the site in the base of the Triangle for a larger building may have provided the basis for compromise on both issues. Louis Simon, who was a designer in the office of the supervising architect from 1910 to 1934 and supervising architect in 1934, wrote several years later pointing out:

> The bulk of a building like that designed for the Department of Commerce left little doubt as to its proper position at the base of the Triangle.[46]

While the Commission of Fine Arts was successful in locating the buildings, Moore and the architect members of the commission were taking steps to ensure the commission a major role in the design of the buildings. Shortly after the Public Buildings Act was signed by President Coolidge, Milton Medary wrote to Moore (sending copies to architects William Adams Delano and Abram Garfield) encouraging the commission to take an active part in designing the buildings. Moore, of course, could not have been in greater agreement:

[A]fter the conference with Secretary Mellon the other day Mr. Wetmore said that he proposed to keep near the Commission of Fine Arts for the reason that he had found that the name of the Commission was a term to conjure with. I said to Mr. Wetmore it was quite evident that his office and the Commission of Fine Arts were going to have a great deal to do with each other and that our aims were similar. Therefore I saw no reason why we should not work in the closest harmony, to which he readily assented. As you already know, I am in pretty close touch with [Louis] Simon. . . . The work is so complex and so big that it is going to be very difficult to exercise as much control as one would wish, but my idea is to make the very best possible cut of a complicated situation.[47]

The commission had continuously stressed the desirability of a plan for the entire group of buildings in the Triangle. Secretary Mellon was sympathetic to the idea of using private architects on public buildings, and in October he appointed Edward H. Bennett consulting architectural specialist to the Treasury Department in connection with the public buildings program. Bennett had studied at the École des Beaux Arts, worked with Daniel Burnham on his plans in Manila, San Francisco, and Chicago, and was a former director of the National City Planning Institute. Mellon said Bennett would collaborate with the office of the supervising architect, the Public Buildings Commission, the Commission of Fine Arts, and the National Capital Park and Planning Commission.[48] Bennett began work on a plan for the area from Ninth to Fifteenth streets, about 85 percent of the Triangle today.

Less than a month later, Bennett presented his plan to the Public Buildings Commission at a special meeting, which Moore attended.[49] Bennett assigned Commerce and Justice to the area between Fourteenth and Fifteenth streets and allotted sites to buildings for General Supply, the Archives, Independent Offices, Labor, Internal Revenue Service, and General Accounting. Moore reported to the Commission of Fine Arts on Bennett's plan at the December meeting. He told them it was satisfactory in that it kept the Commerce Department off the Mall,[50] but he was not happy with the general scheme. Plans were made to hold the commission's February meeting in the New York office of Delano and Aldrich. Former architect members Gilbert, Hastings, Platt, Medary, and Louis Ayres, whose firm York and Sawyer was awarded the commission to do the Commerce Building,[51] were in attendance, as were past sculptor members Daniel Chester French, Herbert Adams, and James E. Fraser. The commission's routine business was disposed of during the morning, and after lunch at the Century Club, the members, past and present, considered "the importance of having a well-designed plan for the entire Triangle," which it now seemed likely the government would purchase.[52]

The result of this meeting was a letter sent by Moore on behalf of the commission to Secretary Mellon. The letter suggested a "considerable change in the grouping of the buildings for the Triangle from the plan prepared by Bennett." It proposed giving the Triangle "a treatment similar to the Louvre in Paris, with colonnades, open courts, and arched driveways, and an extended facade for units of a very large building rather than many individual units."[53]

At the April meeting, Louis Simon brought his preliminary plans for the Internal Revenue Service Building, whose site had been extended to cover the blocks between Tenth and Twelfth streets on B Street, for comment and advice. Moore, however, refused to act on the plans, pointing out that the commission must first know what action Mellon would take on Moore's letter. Moore reported that he and Louis Ayres had been in the office of Assistant Secretary Dewey when the letter was brought before him and that both Ayres and Dewey were favorable to the project. "In fact," Moore said, "Mr. Ayres had expressed himself strongly in favor of the proposed new plan for the Triangle in connection with the plans he is preparing for the new Department of Commerce Building." Ayres's approval is hardly surprising, since he had had a hand in formulating the commission's proposal, but as the architect of the Commerce Building, his approval would have counted heavily with Dewey. Dewey told Moore he would bring the matter to Mellon's attention when the secretary returned from Europe.[54]

Actually, according to Moore's *Memoirs*, Moore had visited Mellon before he left for Europe, armed with a sketch drawn by Louis Ayres on a menu card and a book of pictures of Paris. Moore had then presented the commission's ideas in what he termed "the first of many conversations with Secretary Mellon. . . . From the beginning he was interested in the Washington building program."[55]

The letter containing the commission's proposal was then passed on to Bennett, who wrote about it to Dewey: "I shall want to talk this over with you seriously . . . among other suggestions of no great novelty they suggest the engagement of a landscape architect."[56]

Charles Dewey had already conceived the idea of a group of architectural experts to advise the Treasury Department on the public buildings program and to devise an enlarged scheme for the Triangle.[57] In an official memo to Mellon, Dewey, representing the opinion of members of the Commission

of Fine Arts, the National Capital Park and Planning Commission, and the American Institute of Architects attending a meeting at the Treasury Department, wrote that:

> The buildings for the so-called Triangle area should be grouped so as to give a unified treatment of the composition as a whole, with such special treatment at the through streets as further study may dictate. In view of the many basic questions involved in developing a project of this kind—it is recommended that a Board of Architectural Consultants be formed, under the authority of the Act of May 25, 1926, which provides for the employment of advisory services. . . . In appointing the private architects it would be understood that the interest and ability they displayed . . . would suggest the retaining of each of them as designers of one of the buildings composing the group.[58]

Dewey submitted a list of architects drawn up by Bennett that included Louis Ayres, who was already at work on the Commerce Building, Milton Medary, William Adams Delano, John Russell Pope, and Arthur Brown, Jr. Mellon approved the memo and sent letters of invitation to all the architects on the list. Everyone except Pope accepted. (Pope never answered Mellon's letter.[59]) Louis Simon, at work on the Internal Revenue Service Building, was automatically included and became executive officer of the board. Bennett was appointed chairman by Mellon.

The architects served for travel expenses to Washington for meetings, and they advised on plans for buildings throughout the country.[60] Their reward, of course, was a commission to design one of the Triangle buildings.

The Commission of Fine Arts was pleased with the appointments. Moore had known Bennett in connection with Burnham's plan for Chicago, which Moore had written. Ayres, Delano, and Medary were former commission members, as was Pope, who would be reinvited to become a member of the board later by Mellon and accept. Delano was a current commission member at the time of his appointment. Because of this, Delano said he "had some scruples about accepting this appointment, but Mr. Moore, our chairman, urged me strongly to accept—especially as my term on the Fine Arts Commission was nearing its end."[61] Arthur H. Brown, a well-known San Francisco architect, who along with G. Albert Lansburgh had designed the War Memorial Opera House and War Veterans' Memorial Building in that city, was the only member with no past connection to the Commission of Fine Arts. His work, however, marked him as a leading interpreter of the classical tradition in architecture, and, as Moore pointed out, he had been a student at the École des Beaux Arts at the same time as Pope. Moore also noted that Louis Simon had worked in cooperation with the commission since 1910.[62]

The Board of Architectural Consultants held its first meeting on May 23 with an impressive task: to design for a triangular space of over seventy acres a group of buildings to house the various bureaus and departments assigned there by the federal government. The Triangle formed by the intersection of the diagonal Pennsylvania Avenue with B Street running along the Mall was bounded by Fifteenth Street on the west and Sixth Street on the east. It was cut by two diagonals, Ohio and Louisiana avenues, and laced by C, D, and E streets running east to west and numbered streets running north to south. The Triangle had a frontage along B Street facing the Mall of three thousand feet. Along Pennsylvania Avenue, intersected by both east–west and north–south streets, the frontage was cut up and would be difficult to present as a unified grouping of buildings. The diagonal line of Pennsylvania Avenue also formed unevenly shaped building lots. L'Enfant had planned a transept to the main axis at Eighth Street, with a site for a national church or pantheon where the Patent Office is now located. The Senate Park Commission had marked the cross axis by placing two similar buildings with rounded, recessed facades facing each other from opposite sides of the Mall.

Although the 1929 *Report of the Public Buildings Commission* stated that the Triangle "afforded a rare opportunity for a very grand group of monumental buildings so designed and related as to constitute a single great architectural composition,"[63] there were rumblings of criticism and growing discontent with an architecture that borrowed so heavily from European sources and drew so little on what was considered to be uniquely American. American architecture had focused on residential buildings not public architecture. Louis Sullivan had died destitute in 1924; and of Frank Lloyd Wright, Fiske Kimball wrote in 1928: "Abroad Wright is one to conjure with. At home his design for a skyscraper remains unbuilt. The influence of his ideas here is indirect."[64] Commentators such as Lewis Mumford who, writing in 1924, found the use of classical forms, particularly the Roman, "an imperial facade," noted that "since 1910 the momentum of the Imperial Age seems to have slackened a little; at any rate, in architecture, it has lost much of the original energy which had been given it by the success of the Chicago exposition."[65] Critic and landscape architect Elbert Peets aimed his comments directly at the public buildings program. In 1926, Peets complained about the choice of classical architecture for the new government buildings:

> The architectural ideas that shape them will gain thereby a prestige that will inevitably influence subsequent building in Washington and throughout the country. Unfortunately, it looks now as if that prestige will be given to conceptions of architecture and civic art no longer current and valid—as if a phalanx of turgidly formal boxes of sham masonry will be set up, a permanent monument to unlearned lessons.[66]

There was no chance in the capital, in fact, that new or original concepts in architecture would find a place. While criticism of neoclassical architecture would continue to grow as work on the Triangle progressed, the public expressed a desire for monumentality, not originality or experimentation. The patriotism and zeal for Americana that characterized the 1920s would find an outlet in outdoing the European capital cities in beauty and splendor using classical forms to reflect this country's democratic ideals.

An article in *American City* in 1928 concerning the new building program employed the rhetoric that had grown out of Elihu Root's suggestion in 1901 that any new plan for Washington should stress its relationship to the capital's earliest history. The article referred to Washington as the Wonder City of North America.[67] This new form of rhetoric became so prevalent that as late as 1934, a critic would complain about "Washington booster literature" that referred to the capital as "the Paris of America or the city beautiful" and that described the new public buildings in the city in such phrases as "monumental, fitting in grandeur, awe-inspiring in magnitude, imposing, impressive, imperial."[68] The patriotic rhetoric that

traced both the 1901 plan and its architectural style back to Washington and Jefferson was by now entirely natural to Moore. The zeitgeist of the 1920s proved not only receptive but expansive in regard to building a magnificent capital, and Moore and the Commission of Fine Arts had their hands on the machinery that would dictate its form.

The commission was not having as much success achieving an overall plan for the Triangle as it had with building design.[69] Before the appointment of Bennett and the Board of Architectural Consultants, the Public Buildings Commission had placed various buildings on Triangle sites without regard for an integrated plan, leading Elbert Peets to complain that "the Building Commission does not group its buildings, it parks them."[70] Bennett had created a plan for part of the Triangle, but the Commission of Fine Arts did not recommend it to the building commission; Moore's commission sent its own proposal, based on the plan of the Louvre, to Mellon.[71]

Two accounts ultimately surfaced concerning the design of the Triangle. William Adams Delano in a letter to the *Federal Architect* in 1943 told this version:

> Several of the members of the Board of Architectural Consultants made sketches for the general plan. Arthur Brown, Jr., came to stay with me just before the first meeting and together, one hot Sunday afternoon, we made a rough sketch plan of the group which, in essence, after much discussion, was finally adopted.[72]

Charles Moore gives a different version:

> At a public dinner in New York, Louis Ayres, Milton Medary and I were talking about the

new Washington building program. It was agreed that the buildings should recognize the diagonal of Pennsylvania Avenue; that they should be engaged in so far as possible, in order to minimize the number of competing facades; that the cornice line should be uniform; that open spaces and plazas, after the gay fashion of Paris, should be provided. On the back of the menu-card Mr. Ayres drew a rough plan and gave it to me to use as the basis of a talk with Secretary Mellon. . . . The logical scheme tentatively prepared by Messrs. Ayres and Medary for the grouping of the buildings was followed; and a uniform cornice line as established by the Natural History Museum in the Mall was adopted.[73]

Actually, since Medary, Ayres, and Delano had all been present at the Commission of Fine Arts meetings during which the Triangle development had been discussed, especially those meetings in the spring of 1927 when the commission was preparing its alternate plan to Bennett's, it is doubtful that the two sketches were very far apart.

At the early meetings of the Board of Architectural Consultants during the spring and summer of 1927, guidelines were established for certain features of the design, and assignments were made to the selected architects: Independent office buildings to Delano and Aldrich, Labor and the Interstate Commerce Commission buildings to Arthur Brown, and the Department of Justice Building to the firm of Zantzinger, Borie, and Medary. Edward Bennett's firm of Bennett, Parsons, and Frost were given the building at the apex of the Triangle, temporarily assigned to the Coast Guard, and the responsibility for landscaping. Simon was already at work on the Internal Revenue Service Building and Ayres on the Department of Commerce Building.

Louis Ayres's guidelines for the Triangle

buildings were followed by the other architects and had a strong influence on the design. Louis Simon, executive officer of the board, sent copies to the architects of sketches by York and Sawyer, which, he said, gave certain "guiding figures, such as level of cornices, belt courses, height of stories."[74] While Simon refers in a letter to "the lines which have been pretty thoroughly laid down by the Board,"[75] Ayres's significant role in the project is supported by the dominance of the Commerce Building at the base of the Triangle and the fact that Ayres had already been working on it for several months when the Board of Architectural Consultants formulated the overall plan.[76]

The Triangle buildings adopted a uniform cornice line—also a feature linking the buildings at the Chicago exposition. The height of the buildings was dictated by both the laws of the District of Columbia[77] and the surrounding buildings. Moore expressed special concern over this, first suggesting that the height of the Commerce Building be the same as the Treasury Building.[78] He later appeared anxious that both the height and the architectural style of the National Museum be taken into consideration, which members of the board assured him had been done.[79]

The preliminary plans for the Commerce Department and Internal Revenue Service buildings were submitted for the comment and advice of the commission at its September 1927 meeting. Commissioners in attendance beside Moore were architects Delano, Abram Garfield, and Benjamin Morris (Medary's term had expired) and landscape architect Ferruccio Vitale.[80] Ayres was there in person to present his plans, Simon was not. Board member Arthur Brown attended as a guest.

To accommodate the extraordinary size required by Hoover, Ayres devised three rectangular buildings connected above two gateways by an unbroken structural mass running the length of the buildings. Ayres told the commission that the Commerce Building's six interior courtyards were wide enough to be well-lighted and airy and that he had convinced federal officials that they should be kept clear of all service structures such as garages. The building had a framework of steel and concrete; nevertheless, Ayres had provided seventy Doric columns to decorate the building's four facades. Above the cornices, Ayres had designed a Renaissance balustrade, a feature that would be picked up in adjacent Triangle buildings. The pasting of a classical, or "imperial," as critics would refer to it, facade on a building, whose method of construction did not require it, would be subject to increasing criticism. It did not disturb the Commission of Fine Arts, however; Ayres had included in his estimate of building costs provision for sculpture in the building's four pediments and for a series of relief panels, and engaged a past commission member, James E. Fraser, to design them and supervise their execution.

In a rare instance of self-conscious questioning during the discussion that followed Ayres's presentation, Abram Garfield asked about omitting the columns. Delano answered Garfield's remarks by saying that the board had considered it but felt the columns were needed to break the monotony of the facade and that while they might be omitted in a modern office building, they "have their place in a monumental department building." Ayres then showed a plan of the building designed for Commerce and Labor in 1910 showing simply pilasters. "All admitted, the pilasters gave an ordinary appearance to the building." The plans for the Commerce Department Building were unanimously approved.[81]

William Delano, who wore two hats at the meeting—a voting commission member and a member of the Board of Architectural Consultants—reported that the board members were satisfied with the general scheme of the Federal Triangle and that Mellon, Dewey, and Smoot had agreed to the proposed plan.[82]

The plan described by Delano provided for long exterior facades with great arches and spacious interior courts. One of the interior courts, the Great Plaza between the Department of Commerce and the Post Office, was to be as large as Lafayette Square, and the other, a proposed circular court greater in diameter than Place Vendome in Paris. The plans for the Internal Revenue Service Building were also approved with certain suggested modifications to be communicated to Louis Simon, who was now chief of the architectural division of the office of the supervising architect. The commissioners wanted changes in the archway of the building that was adjacent to the proposed circular court.[83]

The overall designs for the Triangle buildings were not resubmitted to the commission for another two years. The commission, however, was kept well informed by William Delano, Milton Medary, and Louis Ayres. The meeting of the commission in February of 1928 was held in New York City, where the members were the luncheon guests of Mr. and Mrs. Delano. In the evening, they all went to Cass Gilbert's home, where Col. U. S. Grant III and former commission members Herbert Adams, Edwin Blashfield, James E. Fraser, William Mitchell

Kendall along with Ayres, Hastings, and Pope joined them. According to the minutes of the meeting, they discussed the public buildings program.[84] The inner circle thus remained informed and was free to offer suggestions to those members of the board in attendance.

On April 25, 1929, Andrew Mellon invited the Commission of Fine Arts and members of the AIA who were in town for its annual convention to view the model for the Triangle at an evening reception at the Chamber of Commerce. The overall theme of the night was the development of the U.S. Capitol, and the plans for the enlargement of the Capitol grounds, the development of Union Station Plaza, and the Municipal Center, a model of proposed development on the northern side of Pennsylvania Avenue, prepared by the Chicago chapter of the AIA.[85] The 1901 models were also on display that evening.

The Commission of Fine Arts had viewed the Triangle model, which was twenty-two feet long and nine feet wide at the base, earlier in the day, and while impressed, the commission felt that "certain improvements could be made in the model," which it would consider at a future meeting.[86] That evening, however, was a time for congratulations not critiques. The speakers were Treasury Secretary Andrew Mellon, President Herbert Hoover, chairman and vice-chairman of the Public Buildings Commission, Senator Reed Smoot and Representative Richard Elliott, and Milton Medary.

All of the speakers talked of the founding fathers and L'Enfant's plan, and of the importance of new buildings meeting the needs of the federal government. Mellon remembered the 1905 AIA dinner with President Roosevelt, Joe Cannon, and Elihu

Root. He paid tribute to Edward Bennett and the Board of Architectural Consultants and to the cooperation of the Commission of Fine Arts, and "its able and devoted chairman, Mr. Moore." President Hoover's speech showed he shared the bias of the Commission of Fine Arts as well as its rhetoric. He told the audience: "The founders of the Republic also gave us a great tradition in architecture. In after years we have held to it in some periods and in others we have fallen away from it." Hoover then mentioned the excesses of the State, War, and Navy Building but said he had been advised that it could be stripped and brought into harmony with its intended prototype, the Treasury Building. Senator Smoot again expressed his desire to make Washington "the most beautiful capital in the world."[87] A movie prepared under the direction of David Finley at the Treasury Department traced the development of Washington from L'Enfant to the present—emphasizing, in a fashion similar to the Commission of Fine Arts *Annual Report*, the 1901 plan and the progress made in realizing its various features. The present blight along Pennsylvania Avenue was shown along with film clips of the model itself.[88]

A reception the following day was presided over by Charles Moore. As he stood before the guests that evening Moore must have had mixed emotions. He had charted the course of the public buildings program, and although he had compromised, he had won general adherence to the 1901 plan.[89] Now should have been the time to enjoy his tribute to McKim and Burnham. Yet Moore had seen the model and knew it was far from perfect.

In his speech that evening, Moore looked to the past, but unlike the speakers of the evening before, he did not mix nostalgia with the future of Pennsylvania Avenue.

He recalled that snowy night in January 1902 when the Senate Park Commission hosted official Washington to display the models of its plan. He spoke of "the quest for good order and beauty made incarnate in the national capital," and of those "who have come forward in time of peril to do battle for the unity, the dignity, the beauty of the Capital of the United States." Revealing his own feelings toward a battle or two, he said: "There is a fascination in the fray—something akin to the lure of the crusaders to rescue the Holy City from the infidel. It means thought and time and patience and rebuffs and misrepresentation of motives, but it is worth the sacrifice."[90]

While Moore reminisced, Edward Bennett, another of the evening's speakers, described the plan itself:

> Department buildings are to be placed along the south side of Pennsylvania Avenue from the Treasury to the Capitol. In addition to facing on Pennsylvania Avenue these buildings will face also on a grand boulevard[91] which is to be cut through the city, bordering the Mall and stretching from the Capitol to the new Memorial Bridge on the Potomac near the base of the Lincoln Memorial. It is intended the buildings, while having each a separate and distinct architectural treatment, shall be of harmonious design and grouped around two large interior courts or plazas, somewhat after the treatment of the Louvre in Paris.[92]

A central, circular court at Twelfth Street, Bennett explained, would be pivotal to the entire composition. It was proposed to have a great memorial column there. "Vistas," he continued, "will extend from this circular plaza . . . into the other plazas, and especially into the Great Plaza, which . . . opens through an arched way onto Pennsylvania Avenue and the Mall." Bennett also pointed out that L'Enfant did not have compositions lateral to the Mall, though doing so was not out of keeping with eighteenth-century French plans.[93]

The Board of Architectural Consultants had eliminated the diagonals that crossed the Triangle (Ohio Avenue and Louisiana Avenue), the lettered streets running east–west (D and C streets), and Thirteenth Street. The Eighth Street axis had been sealed off by the Justice Department Building,[94] but a shorter Mall transept had been planned, using water and other garden features and terminating in the recessed facade of the Justice Department Building. A similar structure was proposed as a terminus on the opposite side of the Mall. This treatment of the axis derived not from L'Enfant but from the 1901 plan.[95]

NOTES

1. *Washington Star,* August 9, 1923.

2. Charles Moore, "Personalities in Washington Architecture," *Columbia Historical Society Records* 37–38 (1937): 1–15.

3. *Washington Star,* October 16, 1923; October 17, 1923.

4. Commission of Fine Arts. *Minutes,* March 21–24, 1923.

5. *Washington Star,* August 17, 1923.

6. January 11, 1925; reported in the *Washington Post,* January 12, 1925.

7. Commission of Fine Arts. *Minutes,* December 5–6, 1925.

8. *Washington Star,* January 23, 1925.

9. Representative Richard Elliott of Indiana had re-

placed Langley as chair of the House Committee on Public Buildings and Grounds and took his place on the Public Buildings Commission. Other members were Senator Claude A. Swanson of Virginia, Representative Fritz G. Lanham of Texas, David Lynn, architect of the Capitol, James A. Wetmore, acting supervising architect of the Treasury, Maj. U. S. Grant III, director of Public Buildings and Public Parks for the District of Columbia as executive and disbursing officer, and Hugh W. Colton, secretary.

10. *Washington Star*, January 12, 1926; *New York Times*, January 18, 1926. See also *Congressional Record* (April 29, 1926) 69th Cong. 1st Sess., 8484–92.

11. The conditions along Pennsylvania Avenue are pictured in a film, *The Development of the U.S. Capital*, Treasury Department, 1929. Film Collection, National Archives.

12. Charles Moore, *Memoirs*, 311. *Charles Moore Papers*, RG 66, *Records of the Commission of Fine Arts*, National Archives.

13. Grant by dint of this position was executive and disbursing officer of both the Public Buildings Commission and the Arlington Memorial Bridge Commission. Unlike Sherrill who held the position when the title was officer-in-charge of public buildings and grounds, Grant did not become secretary of the Commission of Fine Arts, a post held from 1922 to 1954 by a civilian, H. Paul Caemmerer. In 1942, Grant, now a brigadier general, was named to head the National Capital Park and Planning Commission. His relationship with Moore, while at times strained, was generally cordial. He was a frequent guest of the Commission of Fine Arts at luncheons and dinners, and he and his wife (Elihu Root's daughter) entertained the commissioners on several occasions.

14. U. S. Grant III, "The National Capital: Reminiscences of Sixty-five Years," *Columbia Historical Society Records* 57–59 (1961): 8.

15. *Washington Post*, April 10, 1926.

16. *Congressional Record* (May 1, 1926) 69th Cong. 1st Sess., 8493.

17. *Washington Star*, May 26, 1926.

18. Ibid.

19. Ibid.

20. Otto Wilson, "Washington's Big Building Program," *Review of Reviews* 74 (November 1926): 497.

21. Commission of Fine Arts. *Minutes*, May 28, 1926.

22. *Washington Post*, October 19, 1925.

23. *Washington Star*, September 24, 1926.

24. *Washington Post*, September 24, 1926.

25. *Washington Star*, November 18, 1926.

26. *Washington Herald*, September 25, 1926.

27. Milton B. Medary to Moore, September 30, 1926. *Project Files*, RG 66, National Archives.

28. Moore to Medary, September 22, 1926. *Project Files*, RG 66, National Archives.

29. Commission of Fine Arts. *Minutes*, May 28, 1926.

30. Commission of Fine Arts, *Annual Report*, 1916–1918 (Washington, D.C., 1918), 15; idem. *Minutes*, September 16, 1926.

31. Commission of Fine Arts. *Minutes*, June 17, 1926.

32. *Washington Star*, July 19, 1926; W. M. Jardine to Reed Smoot, July 3, 1926. *Project Files*, RG 66, National Archives.

33. Commission of Fine Arts. *Minutes*, September 16, 1926.

34. Moore to Medary, July 22, 1926. *Project Files*, RG 66, National Archives.

35. *Washington Post*, September 17, 1926; *Washington Star*, September 17, 1926.

36. Moore to Medary, July 22, 1926. *Project Files*, RG 66, National Archives.

37. Commission of Fine Arts. *Minutes*, September 16, 1926.

38. *Washington Post*, September 18, 1926.

39. Charles Dewey, a Chicago banker, served from 1924–27.

40. Lanham, Wetmore, Lynn, and Grant, who was acting chairman.

41. Moore to Medary, September 22, 1926. *Project Files*, RG 66, National Archives; *Washington Post*, September 17, 1926.

42. *Washington Post*, July 16, 1926, October 13, 1926;

Washington Star, September 11, 1926, October 13, 1926.

43. Moore to Medary, September 22, 1926. *Project Files*, RG 66, National Archives.

44. *Washington Post*, September 16, 1926.

45. Moore to Medary, July 22, 1926. *Project Files*, RG 66, National Archives.

46. Louis Simon, "Development of Proposed Federal Building Group at Washington," *Journal of the American Institute of Architects* 16 (February 1928): 63.

47. Moore to Medary, July 22, 1926. *Project Files*, RG 66, National Archives.

48. *Washington Post*, October 22, 1926; *Washington Herald*, October 21, 1926.

49. The meeting was held November 17, 1926.

50. Commission of Fine Arts. *Minutes*, December 2, 1926.

51. *Washington Star*, February 7, 1927.

52. Commission of Fine Arts. *Minutes*, February 5, 1927.

53. Commission of Fine Arts. *Minutes*, April 14–15, 1927.

54. Ibid.

55. Moore, *Memoirs*, 312.

56. William E. Bennett to Dewey [date illegible but received April 27, 1927]. Series 31, General Correspondence and Related Records, 1910–39. *Records of the Public Buildings Service*, RG 121, Washington National Records Center, Suitland, Md.

57. William A. Delano, "A Letter from Mr. William Adams Delano," *Federal Architect* (January–April 1943): 19. In *Project Files*, RG 66, National Archives.

58. Dewey to Andrew Mellon, May 12, 1927. Series 31, General Correspondence and Related Records, 1910–39. *Records of the Public Buildings Service*, RG 121, Washington National Records Center, Suitland, Md.

59. Delano, "A Letter from Mr. William Adams Delano," 19.

60. Charles Dewey said in an interview with the author in his home in Washington, D.C., that his reason for wanting a board of architectural consultants was to shield Mellon from requests from Congress for special favors in appointing architects throughout the country in connection with the general public buildings program. This is also recorded in Dewey's unpublished memoir, "As I Recall."

61. Delano, "A Letter from Mr. William Adams Delano," 19.

62. Moore, *Memoirs*, 313.

63. Public Buildings Commission, *Annual Report*, 1929. S.D. 142, 71st Cong. 2d Sess. (Washington, D.C., 1930).

64. Fiske Kimball, *American Architecture* (New York, 1928), 200.

65. Lewis Mumford, *Sticks and Stones* (New York, 1924; 2d ed. 1955).

66. Elbert Peets, "The New Washington," *American Mercury* 8 (August 1926): 449. Peets, a landscape architect, was a witty and deliberate critic of the landscape establishment as represented by the Commission of Fine Arts and its supporters. He later served on the commission, though that was long after Moore's retirement.

67. John Leo Coontz, "L'Enfant's Dream of Washington Coming True," *American City* 38 (February 1928): 79.

68. William Harlan Hale, "The Grandeur That Is Washington," *Harper's Monthly Magazine* 168 (April 1934): 560.

69. Commission of Fine Arts. *Minutes*, September 16, 1926; May 28, 1926.

70. Peets, "The New Washington," 451.

71. Bennett records in his diary on May 9, 1927, that before the first meeting of the Board of Architectural Consultants, Mellon asked him what he thought of a Louvre treatment for the Triangle. William A. Delano reporting on the early meetings of the board said that the board had been appointed "to make a restudy of the Triangle with a view to giving it a treatment similar to the Louvre as had been recommended by the Commission of Fine Arts rather than many individual buildings." Commission of Fine Arts. *Minutes*, May 27–28, 1927.

72. Delano, "A Letter from Mr. William Adams Delano," 19.

73. Moore, *Memoirs*, 312, 314.

74. Louis Simon to Delano, July 13, 1927. Series 31, General Correspondence and Related Records, 1910–39. *Records of the Public Buildings Service*, RG 121, Washington National Records Center, Suitland, Md.

75. Simon to Louis Ayres, July 16, 1927. Series 31, General Correspondence and Related Records, 1910–39. *Records of the Public Buildings Service*, RG 121, Washington National Records Center, Suitland, Md.

76. Henry Hope Reed gives Ayres credit for fixing the cornice height and for choosing orange-red tiles for the roofs. In Henry Hope Reed, *The Golden City* (Garden City, N.Y., 1959), 96.

77. A 1910 law limited the height of buildings in the District to a maximum of 130 feet.

78. Commission of Fine Arts. *Minutes*, September 16, 1926.

79. Commission of Fine Arts. *Minutes*, September 28, 1926.

80. Not in attendance were H. Siddons Mowbray, painter, and Lorado Taft, sculptor.

81. Commission of Fine Arts. *Minutes*, September 28, 1927.

82. Ibid.

83. Ibid.

84. Commission of Fine Arts. *Minutes*, February 6, 1928.

85. These plans had been shown to the National Capital Park and Planning Commission and the Commission of Fine Arts for their opinions. The NCPPC had apparently viewed them favorably; the Commission of Fine Arts was noncommittal. Commission of Fine Arts. *Minutes*, April 25, 1929.

86. Ibid.

87. Charles Moore, ed., *The Development of the United States Capital* (Washington, D.C., 1930), contains the text of all the speeches given at the reception, which was held on two successive evenings, April 25 and 26, 1929. The quotes are on pages 16, 19–20, and 23.

88. Treasury Department film *Development of the U.S. Capital*.

89. The concentration of the buildings in the Triangle model was much greater than that allowed in the 1901 model. The 1929 version of Triangle development also eliminated the diagonal Louisiana Avenue, which the 1901 plan had not done. It is possible that Moore's desire to protect the Mall from construction of departmental or office buildings may have led him to accept the higher concentration in the Triangle.

90. Moore, ed., *The Development of the United States Capital*, 57.

91. Constitution Avenue.

92. Quoted in Moore, ed., *The Development of the United States Capital*, 66.

93. Moore, ed., *The Development of the United States Capital*, 65.

94. The National Archives was built in the area outlined in the 1901 plan for the Justice Department Building.

95. Commission of Fine Arts, *Eleventh Annual Report* (Washington, D.C., 1929), contains photographs of the 1929 model and plan for the Triangle.

CHAPTER V

BUILDING THE TRIANGLE

1930–37

Whchen the rosy glow of Andrew Mellon's reception had worn off, Moore and the Commission of Fine Arts expressed their unhappiness with certain parts of the scheme. Their dissatisfaction increasingly centered on the work of the chairman of the Board of Architectural Consultants, Edward Bennett. "There is no question," said Moore, "that the Commission of Fine Arts must take the matter in hand and straighten out and complete the model."[1] Nearing the apogée of its power and influence, the commission was able to exercise control and bring about modifications of the Triangle design during the next five years. In doing so, it also impeded progress and left the Triangle vulnerable to growing opposition and competing priorities that would characterize the 1930s.

The commission discussed the model unofficially at the first meeting following the April reception. Benjamin Morris criticized it because it seemed to him to have been done "in commission form." Morris felt that if the scheme could be turned over to one very able designer, it might result in the unification of the whole composition. Moore answered Morris by explaining that "Mr. Bennett, as chairman of the Board of Architectural Consultants, is supposed to be the man who is to do this unifying, but Mr. Bennett has not had the experience of a great architect to do this."[2] Moore pointed out that former commissioners Gilbert, Kendall, and James L. Greenleaf, a landscape architect, "were all critical of the composition."[3]

The commission members found problems with the design of the Justice Department Building and the Archives Building and felt that details of the architectural composition needed attention and that parts of the model were not properly related to each other or to the surrounding area. They noted especially that the District Building should be brought into the scheme but that the old Post Office, whose bulk cut off half of the circular court, should not. In the model, a wing of the Internal Revenue Service Building occupied the ground on which the old Post Office stood; the wing formed the eastern half of the circular plaza and extended as far as Pennsylvania Avenue. Essentially, Benjamin Morris said, the model needed a unified treatment.

> The model [should] be placed in the hands of a great architect like John Russell Pope who would put freshness into the model, and at the same time adhere to classical motives. As a former member of the Commission and acquainted with the Washington development Mr. Pope would also relate the model for the Triangle to the plan of the National Capital.[4]

Pope, of course, had been with the commission for some of its discussion on the public buildings program.

No official recommendations would be made until the model was submitted for the commission's approval in September, two years after the commission had approved the scheme in concept. All of the members of the Board of Architectural Consultants attended the meeting, including Clarence C. Zantzinger who had replaced his late architectural partner, Milton Medary, on the board.[5]

Bennett explained to the commission that Mellon had wanted the Triangle "varied and interesting" but critics had found the uniform building style monotonous. "For this reason," Bennett pointed out, "circles, plazas, domes, and pediments have been introduced into the scheme, . . . presenting

real difficulties."[6] The Board of Architectural Consultants withdrew for the moment and the commission discussed the new plans and prepared its report.

The commission approved Delano's plans for the building to house independent offices and Brown's plans for the Labor and Interstate Commerce Commission buildings. The general plan for the Justice Department was approved, and it was noted that its design was in accord with the 1901 plan. The Pennsylvania Avenue facade was to be restudied, however. Commissioners were dissatisfied with the height of the Archives Building and wanted John Russell Pope called in as architectural adviser. They felt that the central motif of the Great Plaza should be considered to prevent a feeling of crowdedness.[7]

It was becoming apparent that the features of the plan under the direction of Bennett were going to be the ones that were going to have trouble winning commission approval. The individual buildings by the other architects, all past commission members but Brown and Simon, were quickly approved; the features of the overall composition, given to Bennett's firm, were to become the target of continued opposition by the commission, and the commission's relationship with Bennett would steadily deteriorate.

Mellon again wrote to Pope inviting him to serve on the board. Pope answered promptly, enthusiastically offering his services.[8] Pope thus became the seventh member of the board, two years after its formation and after the major features of the Triangle design had been approved.

The Board of Architectural Consultants had its logistical problems that ultimately compromised its effectiveness. Just getting members together to pass on the various features of the plan or getting government accountants to reimburse expenses or switching meeting dates was enough to complicate or prolong the process. Arthur Brown, for example, had great difficulty getting to Washington, and Bennett, who was to be paid by the hour for his administrative work as chairman, waited as long as three years for these relatively modest payments.[9] Of course, reaching a consensus among the board members was a great task since each architect had his own ideas. William A. Delano recorded: "That this group brought order out of chaos is a miracle for there were many more ideas than there were members of the Board and these ideas differed widely."[10] Bennett's job as chairman was not made easier by the fact that Moore was kept informed of the proceedings by Ayres, Pope, and Delano, and when disagreements were reported, Moore took sides and planned strategy for influencing the decision.

One of the first such major problems involved the eastern terminus of the Great Plaza. Arthur Brown had responsibility for the building facades surrounding the plaza, but Delano had responsibility for the building that formed the eastern terminus of the plaza and that was meant to house independent offices. His design had to meet the difficult task forming the eastern end of the rectangular plaza and the western side of the circular court. The desirability of having a motif at the eastern end of the plaza as a dominant element had been discussed at the early meetings of the board. Brown favored a great arch and pediment for that facade, but Delano felt that a large motif made his building seem wasteful and out of scale.[11] Delano designed the side of his building that faced on the plaza as an unbroken colonnade. Bennett attempted to resolve the

matter and to guide opinion on the board toward the solution proposed by Brown.[12] At one point, Delano and Brown were asked to furnish sketches of designs representing the other's point of view.[13] The matter, however, remained undecided, and the model was made in two designs that could be interchanged.[14]

At the November meeting in 1929, a design based on Brown's concept was submitted to the Commission of Fine Arts. The commission had previously expressed dissatisfaction with that design and at this meeting did not approve it. The commission pointed out that the building was meant to house independent offices and the design would lead one to think it housed one of the great departments of the government. The commission then recommended a return to the simpler treatment of the original design—which was Delano's.[15]

Simon forwarded Moore's letter of disapproval to Mellon with a cover letter that maintained that the majority of the Board of Architectural Consultants wanted a "strong accent there."[16] Moore, however, who obviously knew of the disagreement among the board members, had written a confidential letter to Ferry Heath, who had been appointed by Mellon as assistant secretary of the Treasury to take charge of the building program, in which he said he "had reason to believe that if the Board of Architectural Consultants should be polled a majority would be found to agree absolutely with the Commission of Fine Arts."[17] As relations between Moore and Bennett became strained, Heath would increasingly act as an intermediary. Heath then wrote to Moore and said the building slated for independent offices would now be assigned to the Post Office Department.[18] Had the commission's opposition been based solely on the inappropriateness of Brown's design for a nondepartmental building, and not, as it surely was, on a desire to support friend and excommissioner Delano, the matter might have ended there. It did not.

In February of the following year at Mellon's insistence, the commission and the board met together to discuss the east end of the plaza. Moore and the commission did not yield their position but maintained that if a department were to be housed in the building, "a new study would be required."[19] Early in March, Bennett, in a teeth-gritting letter, informed Moore that following the meeting, "the Board talked the thing over and then decided to follow your suggestion with regard to making a plan related to the Post Office Department."[20] Moore wrote at this time to former commissioner James L. Greenleaf, of New York: "We are in the midst of a great struggle with the Treasury architects over certain features of their plans, and so far have been able to hold our own."[21]

Moore meanwhile adopted a different tack. In early March, he wrote to Mellon pointing out that the elaborate pediment proposed for the plaza side of the building did not match the simpler pediment designed by Delano for the other side of the building, which was the principal front and had already been approved by the commission. The building, explained Moore, has two fronts designed separately and "when put together they [do] not fit." He also told Mellon that the hemicycle designed by Delano combined charm and dignity and that the commission "will give it immediate approval."[22]

Mellon sent Moore's correspondence off to Bennett with a letter telling him to accept Delano's design or restudy the other scheme.[23] The Commission of Fine Arts returned two alternate schemes submitted to it

with adverse comments. In April, Simon wrote to Mellon recommending Delano's scheme, which the commission then approved on April 22.[24] Bennett accepted Delano's design but turned it over to Brown to "bring the Plaza into harmony."[25] The result was Delano's simple uninterrupted facade design flanked by two small pediments.

It was apparent, however, that Bennett could not exercise control over the board and with what support he might receive from Brown and Simon could not resolve disagreements when they occurred. Ayres, Delano, and now Pope could seek recourse through Moore and the Commission of Fine Arts. It was also becoming increasingly evident that Mellon would take a personal interest in the Triangle development and would champion the decisions of Moore and the commission. For example, Moore records that after the commission had rejected a particular plan, Mellon sent for Moore to ask if a compromise could not be reached. Moore assented "with reservations," and Mellon replied: "I see that your idea of a compromise is that we accept the advice of the Commission of Fine Arts!" "Admitting the soft impeachment," wrote Moore, "I told him that in his office was an alternative plan which on submission would be returned within a half an hour—approved. It was."[26]

The board located the Oscar Straus Memorial Fountain outside the Triangle, opposite the Fifteenth Street facade of the Commerce Building.[27] Moore pointed out to Mellon the commission's historic opposition to clearing the wooded area south of the Treasury and west of the State, War, and Navy Building (now the Old Executive Office Building). Moore's suggestion that the fountain be placed east of the Fourteenth Street facade of the Commerce Building in the Great Plaza intruded sharply into Bennett's area. His firm had designed the land-scaping for the Great Plaza, including a central reflecting pool. It was two years before the matter was resolved, but Mellon and President Hoover backed Moore's placement of the fountain.[28]

The most drastic alteration in the original model was the change of location of the Archives Building. Early in 1930, John Russell Pope put two designs before the Commission of Fine Arts for the Archives Building: one for the proposed site between Ninth and Tenth streets, the other for the cross axis site at Eighth Street, which was occupied in the model by the Justice Department Building.[29] Pope then suggested that the Archives Building be put on the cross axis site, and the idea received Moore's support.[30]

Pope's design for the building on the Eighth Street axis was neoclassical, with walls punctuated by windows only on the Pennsylvania Avenue side to accommodate offices. According to Moore, it reflected McKim's concept of what the Archives should be.[31] Pope then adorned the building with seventy-two Corinthian columns, each fifty-two feet high, grouped in colonnades and unified on the Constitution Avenue and Pennsylvania Avenue sides by great pediments. A central steel shaft was to hold the records. The decision to single out the Archives, which in the model had been simply a member of the group, and place it at the head of the cross axis represented a major change from the original concept of a grouping of interrelated buildings. Pope was now free to design the building as an individual work and without the constraints of following the diagonal of Pennsylvania Avenue. (Pope, who had not been part of the board when the original scheme was conceived, more than any of the other architects

on the board wore the mantle of the great architect and likely never intended merely to design part of a grouping but rather an individual building.)

Moore's support of Pope could easily have been based on faith in him as a great artist, who, like Burnham and McKim, was larger than life, or on personal loyalty to a past commissioner, which had undoubtedly motivated his support of Delano. It certainly would not have bothered Moore to recommend a change in a scheme for which Bennett had overall responsibility. Moore did however find support for a reinterpretation of the cross axis from an unlikely source—Elbert Peets, who would be the Triangle's most enduring and astute critic. Peets had in fact focused on two major problems of the Triangle design: its noncompliance with the L'Enfant plan and the "conspicuous lack of symmetry and block plan beauty in [the] buildings [that] will make them forever a blemish in the air view of Washington." Peets particularly singled out the Justice Building as an example of the "internally lopsided" design he deplored.[32]

In regard to the L'Enfant plan, which Peets accused the commission and others of lauding in public while cutting up in private, Peets noted that the placement of the Justice Department Building on Eighth Street blocked an important vista, and its lopsided shape (following the diagonal of Pennsylvania Avenue) cut into a square planned by L'Enfant at the midpoint of Pennsylvania Avenue.[33]

Peets's criticism among the general enthusiasm for the building program did not go unnoticed, but it was Charles Moore who answered it. In the *Washington Sunday Star,* eight days before Pope proposed the location change for his Archives Building, Moore made no attempt to discredit Peets's arguments. He simply paraphrased and quoted him at length: thus bringing Peets's remarks to the attention of Washington readers who may have missed them in the Baltimore paper.[34] To Moore, the L'Enfant plan was a public sacred cow used mainly to gain adherence to the 1901 plan, which had supposedly restored L'Enfant's design. (The 1901 plan had also placed a building on the Eighth Street axis, closing off an important vista, but that building had not followed the diagonal of Pennsylvania Avenue, and thus did not cut into the area of L'Enfant's proposed square.) While the 1901 plan did some damage to the L'Enfant design, the 1929 model did more. The fact that Pope's treatment of the cross axis site was closer to that proposed by the Senate Park Commission as well as by L'Enfant would certainly have carried weight with Moore, and Peets's criticisms, considered selectively, were not unwelcome as further support for Pope's proposed modifications of the 1929 model.

Bennett's lack of support from the Commission of Fine Arts made his job increasingly difficult. As chairman of the board, Bennett had the major responsibility for problems of lighting and parking. Bennett, the Board of Architectural Consultants, and the Commission of Fine Arts were all agreed that above-ground parking would mar the beauty of the buildings and the courts.[35] By 1932, however, it was apparent that in view of the depression, underground parking would be too costly. Alternate schemes, such as subsurface parking under the Great Plaza, the Ellipse, and the Mall were also scrapped in 1933 because of the cost. Plans for building parking garages north of Pennsylvania Avenue were also considered but never materialized.[36] The Commission of Fine Arts, however, did not actively concern itself with the parking problem, except that it worked to keep the courts and buildings free from outdoor parking lots or large parking garages.

The logistics of bringing the architects together to agree on various features of the plan in time to meet deadlines also caused a great deal of trouble for Bennett. Submission of the designs to the Commission of Fine Arts further slowed the process, and the commission's disapproval or suggested modifications would mean yet another meeting of the board to work on or approve changes before the designs could be resubmitted. For example, it took so long to approve the pylons and kiosks at the Triangle and to settle on a design for the Great Plaza that President Hoover as well as Secretary of the Treasury Andrew Mellon had left office before the matters were resolved. Under a sweeping reorganization instituted by President Franklin Delano Roosevelt, the office of the supervising architect, now headed by Louis Simon, was placed under the procurement division in the public works branch of the Treasury Department, and the Board of Architectural Consultants ceased to be a viable entity.

The plans for the construction of kiosks and pylons around the Triangle to lend unity and coherence to the composition came under the landscaping responsibilities of the firm of Bennett, William E. Parsons, and Harry T. Frost, but after the commission finally approved them, the National Capital Park and Planning Commission early in 1935 protested against them, finding "that they serve no useful purpose and are something of a menace to traffic."[37] W. E. Reynolds, then acting director of procurement, wrote to Moore and asked the commission to reaffirm its stand in favor of their construction,[38] but despite its support, suggesting different locations and a new design,[39] the contracts were cancelled at the end of 1935. The issue of the monumental sculptures would resurface forty years later in the form of Robert Venturi's proposed plan for Pennsylvania Avenue.[40]

The Great Plaza, another of Bennett, Parsons, and Frost's designs, would meet a similar fate. Bennett showed the commission a preliminary sketch for comment at its meeting in May 1932, and the commission predictably felt the plan should be given considerable further study. In March 1933, the sketches were submitted officially by Bennett, and the commission found them much improved and pronounced them satisfactory. Bennett's design included a central reflecting pool, balustrades, drives, walks, and steps, with the Oscar Straus Memorial Fountain at the western end balanced by a monument at the eastern end. Gilmore D. Clarke, the landscape architect member of the commission, was critical of the planting and asked that a recognized landscape architect be brought in to collaborate. Before giving further advice, however, the commission asked to see a detailed plan showing the driveways and their connections with adjacent streets.[41]

Moore then corresponded with U. S. Grant III, executive and disbursing officer of the National Capital Park and Planning Commission (NCPPC), and pointed out that there were certain problems with the drives and asked if the NCPPC had been consulted. Grant responded that they had not been consulted,[42] and Moore, when he received the drawings from Bennett, sent them to the NCPPC. Charles Eliot of the NCPPC contacted the Commission of Fine Arts, saying the plans were not satisfactory, and his commission needed more information from Bennett, Parsons, and Frost before it could

approve them.[43] Grant found the ramps to be hazardous and an intolerable obstacle to traffic.[44]

At the suggestion of Frederic Delano, chairman of the NCPPC, a joint meeting of the two commissions was held in his office in November 1933. It was decided that a further study of the Great Plaza was needed and that the plaza itself should be simplified, allowing greater accessibility to the public and omitting the reflecting pool. The joint report was sent to Lawrence W. Robert, Jr., assistant secretary of the Treasury.[45] Robert responded by asking for a meeting with NCPPC, the Commission of Fine Arts, and the Board of Architectural Consultants. Again one of Bennett's designs was taken out of his hands.

The meeting was held in January 1934. John Russell Pope, Gilmore Clarke, and Henry V. Hubbard of Harvard's School of City Planning had earlier agreed on a sunken panel to replace the pool. Moore apparently did not agree at first but withdrew his objections in deference to the unanimity among the "experts."[46] The group approved the substitution of a panel, flanked by a balustrade and planted with trees.[47]

The plans for the Great Plaza, however, were never brought to fruition. Early in 1935, Gilmore Clarke wrote to Moore and told him he found the overall plans for landscaping the Triangle prepared by Bennett's firm monotonous and uninteresting.[48] Moore and Clarke were successful in having the planting halted, and a young landscape architect working under Louis Simon was asked to take over.

Both Clarke and Moore began to fear that the plaza would be scrapped altogether and the area turned into a parking lot.[49] The depressed economy and New Deal programs were making inroads into Moore's power and influence over artistic matters in the capital and thus threatening the Great Plaza. Moore was worried even in September of 1935 when he wrote to Simon asking: "Can this [the Great Plaza] be stirred up now?"[50] Simon responded simply that the "comments and advice of the Commission have been carefully noted and appreciated," and that "consideration will be given the modifications suggested in the design of the Great Plaza."[51] In fact, the Great Plaza became a large parking lot. And, with time, a logic developed to replace the parking lot with a building.

Moore did make an effort to reach President Roosevelt on the subject, but his letters on the plight of the Great Plaza and on the sculptures at the entrances to the Arlington Memorial Bridge illustrate his rather cool relationship with the administration. These were not the Coolidge and Hoover days of close cooperation. Moore prepared several drafts of his letters, sending them to fellow commissioners Gilmore Clarke and John Mead Howells for their approval. The final versions, stripped of any remarks even slightly critical,[52] elicited a noncommittal response from Roosevelt, who told Moore the supervising architect of the procurement division of the Treasury Department had been asked to submit estimates through proper channels.[53] There is no doubt that the attitude of the Commission of Fine Arts and Moore toward Bennett and the work of his firm, which prolonged the work on the plaza indefinitely, left it vulnerable to growing space pressures and resulted in its never being completed.

The Apex Building, the only building design in the Triangle awarded to Bennett's firm, came very close to suffering the same fate as the pylons and kiosks. Moore, however, while insisting on certain modifications

(which he had required on all Bennett's work), actively supported its construction.

Opposition to the Apex Building began in 1933. Its proposed tenants had been changed several times: in the early stages of the planning process, it was assigned the Coast Guard; later it was assigned independent commissions, including the Commission of Fine Arts, the National Capital Park and Planning Commission, and the Federal Trade Commission, the agency that actually moved in. The primary argument against the Apex Building was that it would lessen the attractiveness of Pope's neighboring Archives Building. Other considerations were the feeling on the part of Roosevelt that the government must have more space for its money than the Apex design would allow[54] and the possible suitability of that site for the proposed Jefferson Memorial.

The Commission of Fine Arts had approved the design for the Apex Building to house independent offices in December of 1931.[55] Work on the building was not begun, however, and at the end of 1933, President Roosevelt asked the Commission of Fine Arts to investigate protests against the building based on its detraction from the "architectural glory of the Archives."[56] Moore returned that the building had been planned to harmonize with the others in the Triangle and that there was no conflict, recommending to the president that it be built substantially in accord with Bennett's design.[57] Moore then wrote to the architects telling them of his positive recommendation to the president but asking for possible modifications to the building's eastern end and elimination of the building's low extension.[58]

The close coterie of past and present architect commissioners that surrounded Moore was not in agreement concerning the fate of the Apex Building. Commissioner Gilmore Clarke was against it. Past commissioner Cass Gilbert, who was a close personal friend of Moore's, opposed it on the grounds that "the eastern end of the Apex was incapable of solution."[59] The press carried stories of rumors, repeatedly denied, of Pope's opposition to its construction.[60] In January 1934, at a special meeting of the commission attended by former commissioners Pope and Ayres, as well as Chester Aldrich, the commission voted to support the building's design and location.[61] Moore had once again brought the commission to agreement, although it should be noted that Clarke was in the hospital at the time of the meeting.

Bennett, thoroughly unhappy with the Commission of Fine Arts which he referred to as "that most critical court," despite its support for his building, had sought the intervention of Frederic A. Delano, NCPPC chairman. Delano saw President Roosevelt, his nephew, and urged that the Apex be constructed. Roosevelt, however, reportedly wanted to wait and see how things looked after the Archives had been erected.[62]

Moore's support of the Apex Building in this case was not personal; Moore believed the Apex Building acted as a frame for the Archives Building and completed the Triangle in harmony with Pennsylvania Avenue.[63] (Moore later aided the cause of the Apex Building when he advised the Thomas Jefferson Memorial Commission that the Apex location was unsuitable and inadequate for a memorial.)[64]

On May 1, 1936, the commission again approved the design of the Apex Building. The plans had been much revised and were submitted not by Bennett but by Simon.[65] Construction was at last begun, and Presi-dent Roosevelt laid the cornerstone in July of 1937. The Federal Trade Commission moved in less than a year later.

This completed the Triangle as far as possible at that time. The old Post Office and the Coast Guard Building on Pennsylvania Avenue between Twelfth and Fourteenth streets had not yet been razed; the final wing of the Internal Revenue Service Building, which would form the eastern half of the circular court, and the building group forming the northern side of the Great Plaza could not be constructed.[66] There seemed little expectation on Moore's part for any action in the immediate future in regard to further construction, and he announced as early as March of 1937 that "the most extensive public buildings operation ever undertaken by a government has been completed."[67]

During the eleven-year period that had elapsed since the Public Buildings Act passed Congress in 1926, the Commission of Fine Arts had enjoyed unsurpassed prestige and great power. The enactment of the Shipstead-Luce Act in 1930 was a measure both of the commission's acceptance and of its success. The act required plans for private and semipublic buildings to be erected on grounds adjacent to public buildings or on grounds of major importance to be submitted to the commission for its recommendation and instructed the District to "effect reasonable compliance with such recommendation[s]."[68] The bill had been opposed by the District property owners on grounds that it narrowed personal liberties and added to the growing dangers of officialdom,[69] but it was heralded by planners and civic improvement associations as a "most valuable control—protecting the investment of the people of the United States in their public buildings and grounds."[70]

NOTES

1. Commission of Fine Arts. *Minutes*, May 28, 1929, 8.

2. Ibid.

3. Ibid.

4. Ibid., 10.

5. Medary had died in August.

6. Commission of Fine Arts. *Minutes*, September 10–11, 1929, 19.

7. Ibid., 21.

8. Andrew Mellon to John Russell Pope, September 17, 1929; Pope to Mellon, September 30, 1929. Series 31, *General Correspondence and Related Records, 1910–39. Records of the Public Buildings Service*, RG 121, Washington National Records Center, Suitland, Md.

Mellon was miffed that Pope had not answered the first invitation (William A. Delano, "A Letter from Mr. William Adams Delano," *Federal Architect* [January–April 1943]: 19. In *Project Files*, RG 66, National Archives). The two men also shared a mutual acquaintance in Lord Duveen who had chosen Pope to remodel the British Museum and the Tate Gallery. Duveen was Mellon's close friend and adviser on matters of art.

9. In 1934, Bennett applied for payment of $139.64 representing thirty-two and a half hours of work. After numerous letters back and forth, payment was finally made in July 1937.

10. William Adams Delano, "Memoirs of Centurion Architects," in *The Century Association, 1847–1946* (New York, 1947), 214.

11. William Adams Delano to Ferry Heath, assistant secretary of the Treasury, October 28, 1929. Series 31, *General Correspondence and Related Records, 1910–39. Records of the Public Buildings Service*, RG 121, Washington National Records Center, Suitland, Md.

12. Edward H. Bennett, Diaries. December 16, 1928. Unpublished. In the office of Edward H. Bennett, Jr., Chicago.

13. Louis Simon to Delano, November 7, 1928. Series 31, *General Correspondence and Related Records, 1910–*

39. *Records of the Public Buildings Service*, RG 121, Washington National Records Center, Suitland, Md.

14. Simon to Delano, November 10, 1928. Series 31, *General Correspondence and Related Records, 1910–39. Records of the Public Buildings Service*, RG 121, Washington National Records Center, Suitland, Md.

15. Commission of Fine Arts. *Minutes*, November 18, 1929.

16. Moore to Bennett, November 20, 1929; Simon to Mellon, November 30, 1929. Series 31, *General Correspondence and Related Records, 1910–39. Records of the Public Buildings Service*, RG 121, Washington National Records Center, Suitland, Md.

17. Moore to Heath, November 20, 1929. *General Correspondence*, RG 66, National Archives.

18. Heath to Moore, November 25, 1929. In "Report on the Great Plaza," *Project Files*, RG 66, National Archives.

19. Commission of Fine Arts. *Minutes*, February 10, 1930.

20. Bennett to Moore, March 3, 1920. *Project Files*, RG 66, National Archives.

21. Moore to James L. Greenleaf, February 28, 1920, *Charles Moore Papers*, RG 66, National Archives.

22. Moore to Mellon, March 3, 1920; March 5, 1920. Series 31, *General Correspondence and Related Records, 1910–39. Records of the Public Buildings Service*, RG 121, Washington National Records Center, Suitland, Md.

23. Mellon to Bennett, March 6, 1920. Series 31, *General Correspondence and Related Records, 1910–39. Records of the Public Buildings Service*, RG 121, Washington National Records Center, Suitland, Md.

24. Moore to Mellon, April 22, 1930. Series 31, *General Correspondence and Related Records, 1910–39. Records of the Public Buildings Service*, RG 121, Washington National Records Center, Suitland, Md.

25. Bennett to Delano, April 25, 1930. Series 31, *General Correspondence and Related Records, 1910–39. Records of the Public Buildings Service*, RG 121, Washington National Records Center, Suitland, Md.

26. Moore, *Memoirs*, 315.

27. Mellon to Moore, February 18, 1930. Series 31, *General Correspondence and Related Records, 1910–39. Records of the Public Buildings Service*, RG 121, Washington National Records Center, Suitland, Md.

28. James Wetmore to Ferry Heath, November 26, 1932. Series 31, *General Correspondence and Related Records, 1910–39. Records of the Public Buildings Service*, RG 121, Washington National Records Center, Suitland, Md.

29. Commission of Fine Arts. *Minutes*, February 10, 1930.

30. Moore, *Memoirs*, 328.

31. Moore stated: "Mr. Pope professed that he had pondered the words of Charles McKim I often quoted to him—that the Archives was the one building he most wanted to design; he would like to see what he could do with plain walls and the simplest materials." Moore, *Memoirs*, 330.

32. *Sunday Sun* (Baltimore), January 26, 1930. Reprinted in David Speiregen, ed., *On the Art of Designing Cities: Selected Essays of Elbert Peets* (Cambridge, Mass., 1968), 83, 86.

33. Ibid., 79–80.

34. *Washington Sunday Star*, February 2, 1930.

35. Pope to Moore, October 15, 1931. *Project Files*, RG 66, National Archives.

36. Bennett, Diaries, September 21, 1931; October 17, 1931; July 13, 1933.

37. Frederic A. Delano, chair, NCPPC, to Adm. C. J. Peoples, director of procurement, April 17, 1935. *Project Files*, RG 66, National Archives.

38. W. E. Reynolds to Moore, April 6, 1935. *Project Files*, RG 66, National Archives.

39. H. Paul Caemmerer to Reynolds, June 6, 1935. *Project Files*, RG 66, National Archives.

40. Commission of Fine Arts. *Minutes*, March 2, 1978.

41. Commission of Fine Arts. *Minutes*, March 17–18, 1933.

42. Moore to U. S. Grant III, March 28, 1933;

Grant to Moore, April 5, 1933. *Project Files*, RG 66, National Archives.

43. Grant to Harry T. Frost, May 22, 1933. *Project Files*, RG 66, National Archives.

44. Ibid.

45. Commission of Fine Arts. *Minutes*, November 17–18, 1933. Robert served under Treasury Secretary Odgen Mills.

46. Moore to Henry V. Hubbard, December 1, 1933. *Project Files*, RG 66, National Archives.

47. Commission of Fine Arts. *Minutes*, Addendum, December 15, 1933.

48. Gilmore Clarke to Moore, April 10, 1935. *Project Files*, RG 66, National Archives.

49. Clarke to Moore, June 28, 1935. *Project Files*, RG 66, National Archives.

50. Moore to Simon, September 24, 1935. *Project Files*, RG 66, National Archives.

51. Simon to Moore, May 19, 1936. *Project Files*, RG 66, National Archives.

52. A March 30 version of the first letter pointed out that "completion is halted because while great amounts have been expended on them, the comparatively small amounts needed for completion are withheld." The final versions were April 11 and April 20, 1936. *Project Files*, RG 66, National Archives.

53. Franklin Delano Roosevelt to Moore, May 12, 1936. *Project Files*, RG 66, National Archives.

54. Moore to Pope, February 20, 1934. *General Correspondence*, RG 66, National Archives.

55. Moore to Mellon, December 18, 1931. *General Correspondence*, RG 66, National Archives.

56. *Washington Evening Star*, December 13, 1933.

57. *Washington Post*, December 14, 1933; Moore to Roosevelt, December 29, 1933. *General Correspondence*, RG 66, National Archives.

58. Moore to Bennett, Parsons, and Frost, December 19, 1933. *General Correspondence*, RG 66, National Archives.

59. Moore to Pope, February [29], 1934. *General Correspondence*, RG 66, National Archives.

60. *Washington Evening Star,* November 14, 1935.

61. Moore to Roosevelt, January 23, 1934. *Project Files,* RG 66, National Archives.

62. Bennett, Diaries, February [n.d.] 1933; December 27, 1933; January 14, 1934; January 22, 1934.

63. Moore to Roosevelt, January 23, 1934. *Project Files,* RG 66, National Archives.

64. Moore, *Memoirs,* 310.

65. Moore to Simon, May 2, 1936. *General Correspondence,* RG 66, National Archives.

66. The Coast Guard Building has since been demolished, freeing the site for construction of a building group along Pennsylvania Avenue such as outlined by the 1929 models. The old Post Office won a reprieve from the bulldozer, jutting into what was to have been the Triangle's circular court and backing up to the Internal Revenue Service Building whose addition would have extended out to Pennsylvania Avenue.

67. *Washington Star,* March 14, 1927.

68. Public Law 231, 71st Cong., 2d sess., S. 2400.

69. Clipping, n.p., n.d. Commission of Fine Arts file. *Washingtoniana Collection,* Martin Luther King, Jr., Public Library, Washington, D.C.

70. Harlean James, "Architectural Control Now a Fact in Washington," *American City* 43 (July 1930): 148. James was executive secretary of the American Civic Association.

CHAPTER VI

THE TIDE CHANGES

The passage of the Shipstead-Luce Act in 1930 and its enthusiastic reception in professional circles represented a pinnacle for the Commission of Fine Arts under Moore's leadership. As the depression deepened (rather than lifted) in the 1930s, however, and as a Democratic administration replaced the Republicans, the consensus of opinion supporting the commission's goals of the 1920s was breaking down. In the world of architecture, the muffled criticism of the 1920s had become a roar directed against an architecture that was applied archeology, and civic leaders were increasingly rejecting a conception of city planning that built a court of honor rather than dealing with growing urban ills. All of these forces produced an uneasiness that even invaded the upper room of the Century Club when the past and present members of the Commission of Fine Arts gathered for what Moore called a family party. The celebration took place on May 23, 1935, the twenty-fifth anniversary of the commission's creation, and its purpose was to honor Charles Moore, who was now eighty years old.

Moore was given a gold medal designed by sculptor Lee Lawrie[1] of the commission and a portrait of himself by another commissioner, Eugene Savage,[2] showing Moore with the L'Enfant plan before him and the Lincoln Memorial, the Washington Monument, and the Capitol in the background. Of the twenty-eight past commissioners, fourteen were still living; nine were in attendance with the seven present commissioners, and the other five had sent nostalgic letters of mingled regret and reminiscence. Royal Cortissoz, art editor of the New York *Herald Tribune*, was a guest, as was William W. Harts, now a general, and always the favorite of the four army ex-officio secretaries. Elihu Root sent a letter recalling the commission's genesis. Moore observed, "Few persons thought the Commission would survive for a quarter of a century. But it had become an institution." "Instead of derisive jeers that greeted mention of the Commission during its early years," Moore pointed to the fact that legislation regarding art matters uniformly called for the advice of the commission, noting with satisfaction the successful operation of the Shipstead-Luce Act.[3]

It was meant to be an evening recalling the battles and victories of the past, but the present with all its uncertainties intruded into the celebration. Moore records that "an undercurrent of apprehension pervaded the scene." The commission members sympathized with Louis Simon, who as supervising architect had his office engulfed by the procurement division, described by Moore as "1,500 draftsmen making blue-prints in a loft building." It was, said Moore,

> a degradation of the art of architecture that provoked angry expostulation from Louis Ayres and rendered Blashfield, Herbert Adams and Kendall protestingly speechless under the swelling tide of "modernism"; engulfing tradition and training and bring[ing] chaos to the fine arts. . . . Reaction, they assured themselves, would come with the restoration of business confidence and enterprise, necessary to furnish the means of opening closed offices and also to bring a return of public demand for the creations of artists of training, persistence and talent. Meantime the problem was to withstand present adverse conditions. Valiantly Commission men were carrying on.[4]

There would be no reaction away from "modernism," however, when the depression was over. Tastes were changing. The classicism to which these men adhered, with its set rules and its formalized training, had en-

joyed wide acceptance, but now the tide had turned. The Triangle group continued to be on the defensive throughout the 1930s.

Writing in 1932 concerning the public buildings program, Col. U. S. Grant III said the buildings were "designed to combine both the utility and the beauty requisite to efficient and economical administration of the government activities, as well as the dignity and character of the national capital." Grant defended the program as "far from being an extravagant expenditure of funds to obtain attractive buildings," assuring his readers, "it is an absolutely practical measure."[5] While Grant defended the expenditures for monumental buildings in a depression period, Harlean James in 1935 defended the choice of eighteenth-century neoclassical architecture:

> After weighing the present trend toward freedom from the established school of thought against the architectural tradition established in Washington, it was concluded that a violent departure from the dominant note of classical architecture would be unjustifiable. . . . This is the answer to the charge of architectural monotony which has been raised by a critical opposition. Proponents of the Triangle plan believe its architectural unity will provide a sense of harmony which seldom has been possible over so large an area.[6]

James stated that the most serious charge against the Triangle construction is "that the buildings have been designed for their exterior appearance rather than for their functional use" and that a modern office building would have provided better working conditions. Admitting conformity to a uniform architectural exterior plan, James expressed doubt "whether very much better conditions could have been provided in buildings of so-called modern architecture."[7]

Such defenses, however, were unable to hold back the mounting wave of criticism of the Triangle plan. A particularly devastating article appeared in 1934 written by William Harlan Hale. Hale attacked the expense and the architecture of the new buildings and the agency he considered responsible for the whole thing, the Commission of Fine Arts. He pointed out the expense of the entire buildings program at one hundred million dollars. Hale took on the buildings one at a time. He noted that the Commerce Building had a concrete foundation and steel girders but that the architect had still insisted on heavy walls and great colonnades. "Not yet exhausted by the grand total of seventy solid stone columns almost fifty feet in height," Hale complained, "they punched great entrance arches into the walls, and finished off the whole structure with a Renaissance balustrade above the cornices." Hale pointed out the irony that a building erected with the cooperation of Herbert Hoover, the Great Engineer, "simply threw to the winds all the achievements of modern engineering in order to make itself over into a Roman Renaissance palace." Hale continued counting columns, French Renaissance pavilions, and Roman temple porticos throughout the Triangle group noting "how the money goes as the gorgeousness grows."[8]

Hale then asked, "Who is responsible for all this?" He concluded it was the Commission of Fine Arts.[9] Hale described the commission as having from the time of its establishment been captured "by the neo-classical enthusiasts who had made the World's Fair buildings. And . . . in all these years it has never been rescued from the hands of that group and its sworn disciples." Hale accused the commission of seeking "grandeur above all" and ignoring "all modern technique in orientation, ventilation and common-sense

city planning."[10] In a stinging indictment he maintained:

> The Commission of Fine Arts is responsible for the fact that no opportunity was afforded to have those buildings designed and decorated by architects and artists who are trying to bring forth an American idiom rather than carry on the Beaux Arts tradition of miscellaneous imitation. The big commissions have gone to men like Cass Gilbert[11] and John Russell Pope, who design equally brilliantly in all styles that are safely dead, or to Delano and Aldrich, famous for their "period" residences in Westchester and Long Island. There was no place for the decorative ideas of a Frank Lloyd Wright; for the progressive technique of a William Lescaze; for the more conventional but vigorous metropolitan design of a [Raymond M.] Hood or [Harvey Wiley] Corbett; there was no place for the dozens of striving architects and planners who have understood the great Louis Sullivan's statement that "form follows function," and who might have conceived the buildings as organic expressions of what was in them and the great work they were being used for, rather than as ancient mausoleums to hide that work.[12]

The increasing acceptance of Hale's criticism became apparent at a symposium devoted to public buildings and monuments sponsored by the American Federation of the Arts in 1937. The federation's choice of topic had been stimulated by the national debate over the design of the Jefferson Memorial[13] between those who, like Moore, believed that classical forms were the universal language of permanence and beauty and those who found in copying the architectural forms of the past a "betrayal of the artistic integrity of our (the American) people."[14] Moore found few supporters at the symposium. Carl Feiss, professor of planning and housing at Columbia University School of Architecture; Joseph Hudnut, dean of the Graduate School of Design at Harvard; and architect William Lescaze took exception to the development of Washington as "a huge and permanent Fair." They refused to accept the principle that "all growth and all development was to take place strictly within a firm framework adapted once and for all by the men of the late 1890s who were thus to impress their concepts of form upon posterity."[15] They agreed with William Lescaze when he asserted that: "America has definitely outgrown the imitation of Greek or Italian architecture. America is quite capable of developing its own architecture."[16]

That same year, Elbert Peets again attacked the Senate Park Commission plan for doing damage to the L'Enfant plan. He accused its creators of designing "a city-within-the-city," apart from the rest of Washington. L'Enfant, he said, "dreamed not of a beautiful court of honor, but of a beautiful city." Peets described the Triangle as "our national conspicuous waste, our display of superfluous power."[17]

Lewis Mumford's concern for an architectural style that was what he called a mask, or an imperial facade, was shared by an increasing number of commentators. Joseph Hudnut wrote, "How inadequate is the death-mask of an ancient sculpture to express the heroic soul of America."[18] Eventually the AIA would join the chorus of critics, cautioning, as urban redevelopment got under way in 1948, against any repetition of its "facadism" and calling its eclectic style "as boring as it was massive and unoriginal."[19]

The Triangle was criticized for possessing all the failings of the City Beautiful movement. The placement of a large government complex in the center of the city was criticized for adding to the growing problems of traffic and congestion. It intensified the city-within-the-city aspect of monumental Washington, creating an edge between it and vernacular Washington.[20] A grouping of single-use buildings, deserted when the work force was gone, brought sterility to the south side of Pennsylvania Avenue and blight to the north. Nor could the Triangle escape from another charge leveled at the City Beautiful movement—that money was spent on magnificent buildings while the pressing needs of the city went unmet.

The commission, perhaps succeeding too well in its mission, saw itself as going to battle for the welfare of the city. The National Capital Park and Planning Commission created in 1926 was just settling in as plans for the Triangle were being formulated and did not at that time equal the commission in power and influence.

The greatest criticism that can be leveled against the commission, however, is that it was unable to finish building or designing the Triangle. The Federal Triangle by the late 1930s won few plaudits. The new aesthetic of modernism was replacing the older Beaux Arts aesthetic. The modernists viewed the Federal Triangle as the last gasp of the older order. Too much monumentality voids itself, and the Triangle becomes a sea of limestone. The commission's inability to complete the plan added obvious shortcomings. The proposed islands of green, notably the Great Plaza, instead of providing settings for formal facades of the surrounding buildings and areas of serenity for visitors and government employees, are filled with cars. The Triangle along Pennsylvania Avenue from Tenth Street to Fourteenth Street presents a confusion of unfinished facades cut by streets and parking areas. The majority of the buildings lack individual distinction, yet the overall design to which that distinction was sacrificed remains incomplete. The absurdity of Delano's semicircular classical facade facing a dark, uneven corner of the Romanesque old Post Office, which prevents completion of the circular court, is a problem without resolution. In its present state, the Triangle is marked by confusion and a low image, its massiveness is both forbidding and ill-defined.

The characteristics that made the commission as effective as it was were the same that slowed progress on the Triangle, weakened its overall plan, and resulted in its remaining incomplete. These characteristics—a shared bias for classical architecture, institutionalized in academies throughout the country; the strong and continuous leadership of Charles Moore; the personal and professional loyalties of its members; and its refusal to allow dissenting opinion within its closed circle—allowed the commission to dictate location, general plan, style, and architects of the Triangle. Its recommendations became mandates; its disapprovals were tantamount to vetoes. Yet with all this power, the members of the commission were unable to bring about the classical perfection they sought for the Triangle. And the priorities of the New Deal along with realities of the depression, the growing criticism of classic eclecticism in architecture, and Moore's flagging strength—he was eighty-two in 1937—prevented the successful resolution of the commission's problems that politics could not make disappear.

It is possible that even if the commission had pushed Triangle construction along more rapidly under earlier optimum conditions, they could not have brought about the demolition of the old Post Office. The designers of the Triangle felt that it had no place in their classical scheme, and they drew up a plan that required its demolition

for the completion of the central, pivotal circular court. Yet there were no plans for its removal at the time of the Triangle construction. The commission insisted that the District Building be included in the scheme, but its bias against the old Post Office was too great. It sought no modifications to allow for its possible existence within the scheme.

Perhaps the commission can be faulted for excluding from its closed club those who might have brought a freshness of interpretation to the classical tradition, which had become sterile. It was certainly unlikely that in the 1920s the commission would have reached out to an experimentalist, or that the establishment would have accepted such a break with traditional public architecture. But a more open commission might at least have carried on a dialogue about what governmental architecture ought to represent. Charles Moore did, however, as its chairman, provide the link between government and artist, and in this uneasy cooperation ensured that the voice of the artist prevailed. And Moore, through the Commission of Fine Arts, enforced a well-conceived plan on monumental Washington, which for too long had been left to the caprice of Congress, and perpetuated the neoclassical tradition of the city's early years, ensuring its dominance in the capital for many years to come.

The Federal Triangle had long been criticized by modernists attempting to establish a new design aesthetic, by planners trying to establish a professional role for themselves, and by interested citizens concerned about the uncompleted nature of the overall plan or the jarring incongruity of the old Romanesque Post Office standing amidst the circular court that was to be larger than Place Vendome in Paris. Yet, when looking at these buildings, one discovers that they are very good buildings. Their traditional materials have well stood the test of time, something that could not be said of many of the innovative building materials introduced by the modernists. The Triangle buildings' proportions, particularly their interior proportions, reflect a gracious age before the modernists' introduction of the analysis of space and its subsequent minimization to reduce costs. And although accused of sterility, the Federal Triangle buildings seem bold and fascinating compared to what was to follow. But perhaps most important, the people who use these buildings like them and have a great pride in them—the results of the work of the commission and Charles Moore.

Perhaps the best assessment of the power and prestige of the Commission of Fine Arts and the man who personified it for twenty-two years was made by the *Washington Daily News* in reference to the election of Gilmore Clarke, Moore's successor. The *News* commented that "Almost any American artist or architect would rather be Gilmore D. Clarke than be President."[21]

NOTES

1. Lawrie served two nonsuccessive terms on the commission, from 1933 to 1937 and from 1945 to 1950.

2. Savage served on the commission from 1933 to 1941.

3. Moore describes the gathering in his *Memoirs*, 349–53. *Records of the Commission of Fine Arts*, RG 66, Charles Moore Papers, National Archives. The quote is taken from p. 349.

4. Ibid., 352.

5. U. S. Grant III, "The New City of Washington," *Review of Reviews and World's Work* 86 (November 1932): 33–35.

6. Harlean James, "The Washington Triangle Rises," *Review of Reviews and World's Work* 91 (January 1935): 62. James's statement is incorrect in that it assumes that the matter was debated and decided in favor of classical architecture. The uniformity of opinion among commission members and city leaders in 1928, when plans for the Triangle were formulated, made such a debate impossible.

7. Ibid.

8. William Harlan Hale, "The Grandeur That Is Washington," *Harper's Monthly Magazine* 168 (April 1934): 564.

9. Ibid., 566. Hale's statement is quite strong: "The Public Buildings Act of 1926 . . . placed the whole program specifically in the hands of the Secretary of the Treasury, who appointed a Board of Architectural Consultants for expert assistance. In Congress the body representing the building campaign is the Public Buildings Commission. But, behind these organizations and towering over them in its authority in regard to the actual evolution of the plan, is the Commission of Fine Arts."

10. Ibid., 567.

11. Ibid., 565–66. Cass Gilbert was the architect of the Supreme Court Building, which Hale considered most grandiose of all.

12. Ibid., 567.

13. Moore took an active part in the early phases of planning the memorial, particularly the setting of the location. When he retired, however, the design had not been decided, and the commission's position was represented by the incoming chairman, Gilmore Clarke.

14. "Discussion of Public Architecture: Symposium on Public Buildings and Monuments Conducted by the American Federation of Arts," *Architectural Record* 82 (August 1937): 53.

15. Joseph Hudnut, "Classical Architecture Not Essential," *Architectural Record* 82 (August 1937): 54.

16. William Lescaze, "America's Outgrowing Imitation Greek Architecture," *Architectural Record* 82 (August 1937): 55.

17. Elbert Peets, "On the Plans for Washington," in David Speiregen, ed., *On the Art of Designing Cities: Selected Essays of Elbert Peets* (Cambridge, Mass., 1968), 69, 78.

18. Joseph Hudnut, "The Last of the Romans," *American Magazine of Art* 34 (April 1941): 173. See also Hudnut, "Recent Buildings," *Home and Garden* (July 1940): 42ff.

19. Constance McLaughlin Green, *Washington: Capital City, 1879–1950* (Princeton, 1963), 503.

20. See Frederick Gutheim, "City and Capital," *Journal of the American Institute of Architects* (January 1963): 85–90, and "Washington Needs Decentralization," *New Republic* 106 (June 15, 1942): 826–27. See also Alfred Kastner, "The Plan," *House and Garden* (July 1940): 41ff; and Miller McClintock, "Traffic Problems," *House and Garden* (July 1940): 44–45.

21. *Washington Daily News*, October 19, 1937.

EPILOGUE

When Gilmore Clarke became chairman of the Commission of Fine Arts in 1937, the Federal Triangle was essentially complete, but some important business had been left unfinished. This was due largely to a growing reluctance to appropriate more funds for the grandiose project while the depression dragged on. The construction of a building to replace the one occupied by the Coast Guard (between the District Building and the new Post Office Department) had yet to be seriously discussed; plans to demolish the old Post Office had never been realized. Because of the continued presence of this building, the impressive paved and arcaded circle on Twelfth Street, in the center of the Triangle, could not be completed. Because years of indecision had delayed the landscaping of the Great Plaza off Fourteenth Street and because no provision had been made for employee parking, the Triangle's second great open space had become a parking lot.

In 1936, architect Louis Simon made a prophetic statement regarding the Great Plaza: "The longer this place is left as an automobile park, the more difficult it is going to be to change its character."[1] In spite of repeated urgings by the Commission of Fine Arts that the landscaping be completed, Gilmore Clarke was willing, in 1938, to compromise with the National Capital Park and Planning Commission, at that time pressing for some accommodation of cars in the plaza, and allow a limited amount of parking on the drive around the perimeter in exchange for landscaping the central area. But in this time of restricted funds, nothing was done, and World War II put an end to further consideration. Postwar Washington was more and more dependent on the automobile, and Clarke came to realize the hopelessness of the situation. In 1948, he said:

> I feel, as far as speaking for this Commission, that we would rather have a park area there than anything else, a place where the employees can go out in the middle of the day and have a place for recreation. But, on the other hand, we cannot ignore the practical factors of the parking of cars. Unfortunately, it has gotten off to a precedent where they park 1,000 or 1,100 cars there, and it is hard to break that.[2]

Clarke's suggestion to the commissioner of public buildings was to study placing the cars in a depressed central space with trees around the edge and within the parking area itself.

In 1950, a new chairman of the Commission of Fine Arts arrived. He was David Finley, director of the National Gallery of Art and chair of the National Trust for Historic Preservation. Finley was distressed by the eyesore conditions in the Great Plaza and repeatedly discussed the matter with officials of the National Park Service and the NCPPC. He received little satisfaction; the answer was always that there was no place to put the cars. In 1956, the commission agreed to some additional parking in the hemicycle and the Twelfth Street court of the Post Office Department, if the parking were removed from the Great Plaza; again, nothing happened. In 1959, a request from the General Services Administration to repave the plaza for continued use as a parking lot was refused. In 1960, a plea was made to outgoing President Eisenhower, noting that the plaza was on the ceremonial route taken by distinguished foreign visitors on the way to the White House; mention was also made that it was the site of a memorial to Secretary of Commerce Oscar Straus.

During his inaugural parade, John F. Kennedy made his now-famous observation about the dilapidated condition of the north side of Pennsylvania Avenue, and in 1962, the President's Council on Pennsylvania Avenue was established. It concerned itself with the Federal Triangle as well as the rehabilitation of the north side of the avenue. In its first report, issued in 1964, the recommendation in regard to the Triangle was summarized in two words: Finish it.[3] There was agreement with the Commission of Fine Arts that the Great Plaza should be a landscaped park as intended, although the report added that the parking should not be lost but put underground. The Coast Guard Building was to be demolished, and the Triangle completed from the Post Office Department to the District Building. The interior courts of the existing buildings were to be cleared of paraphernalia and automobiles and landscaped as originally planned. The second great open space of the Triangle, the Great Circle at Twelfth Street, was to be completed. This, of course, would require the demolition of the old Post Office, and here the council members were not in total agreement. The question was whether the entire building should go or whether the tower should be retained and incorporated into the new construction as a reminder of the past, an agreeable vertical element on Pennsylvania Avenue, and a place from which tourists could view the city. By majority vote, the members agreed to recommend retention of the tower. The Commission of Fine Arts listened to the council's proposals in October 1963 before the report was released; there were no specific comments on the Federal Triangle part of the plan.

A second Pennsylvania Avenue report was issued in January 1969.[4] It continued to call for the completion of the Triangle with

development but the older Treasury Building, where he took his cue from the grouping of windows between pilasters. The commission reviewed a preliminary landscape plan for the plaza off Pennsylvania Avenue and found that it posed a number of problems. There was a long discussion about the form and detailing of an octagonal element that projected into the plaza; neither the architect nor the commission was satisfied with it. And so the review process goes on.

Other factors may alter the original concept. The estimated cost is staggering—close to seven hundred million dollars. And there have been questions about the International Cultural and Trade Center, whether or not it will be a viable operation. Without this function the building would inevitably assume a different character.

Two other Federal Triangle projects came before the commission at the time it was considering the International Cultural and Trade Center project. In February 1990, architects Karn, Charuhas, Chapman, and Twohey received approval for a primarily glass building that would fit in between the old Post Office and the Internal Revenue Service Building, filling most of the latter's courtyard. In October, the same architects showed preliminary plans for the long-awaited finishing off of the ends of the Internal Revenue Service Building. The work would be carried out in a style similar to but simpler than the original building. The commission was pleased with the design and looked forward to the removal of one of the eyesores of Pennsylvania Avenue.

The Commission of Fine Arts still feels a certain pride of authorship in the Federal Triangle. It is useless to speculate on what Charles Moore would have thought about the concept of a glass building between the Internal Revenue Service and the old Post Office, or the filling in of the Great Plaza with massive construction, but it can safely be said that he would have approved of the new respect for the Triangle's classical revival architecture and that he would have been pleased that the plans were developed in the 1990s rather than the 1960s.

CHARLES H. ATHERTON
Secretary

SUE A. KOHLER
Historian

Commission of Fine Arts

NOTES

1. Commission of Fine Arts. *Minutes*, May 1, 1936, 15.

2. Commission of Fine Arts. *Minutes*, January 14, 1948, 4.

3. *Pennsylvania Avenue: Report of the President's Council on Pennsylvania Avenue* (Washington, D.C., 1964). The Federal Triangle proposals are summarized on p. 37.

4. Ibid., 42–47.

5. Commission of Fine Arts, *Transcript of Meeting, February 25, 1970*, 31.

PHOTOGRAPHS OF THE FEDERAL TRIANGLE

BY JACK E. BOUCHER

The arched gateways and pedimented pavilion of the Inter-
state Commerce Commission Building as seen from the
Smithsonian Institution's National Museum of American
History.

The view from the top of the Commerce Building looking east shows the Interstate Commerce Commission Building on the right and the Ariel Rios Building on the left.

This tympanum sculpture entitled *Commerce and Communications* shows the mythological figure Mercury carried through the sky on horseback as designed by Wheeler Williams and carved on site by the John Donnelly Company.

The principal entrance to the U.S. Customs Service
Agency (formerly the Department of Labor Building) is set
on the west end of the building between two Doric pavilions on Constitution Avenue.

The Departmental Auditorium pavilion, in concert with its
importance in this group of federal buildings, protrudes
from the Constitution Avenue facade.

A massive entablature supported by fluted Doric columns separates the Departmental Auditorium from its neighbors.

Large arched entrances divide the Departmental Auditorium from the neighboring federal buildings, the Interstate Commerce Commission to the east and the U.S. Customs Service Agency to the west.

The largest room in the Departmental Auditorium is the
auditorium itself, which is four stories high and seats
twenty-five hundred people.

Along the south wall of the auditorium above the doors to
the lobby is a splendid stepped platform balcony.

A small meeting room behind the auditorium looks out over the Great Plaza and is decorated in a French neoclassical style with bright green and gold painted accents.

All the lighting in the Departmental Auditorium was designed by Arthur Brown, including these magnificent burnished aluminum and gold-leaf bracket lamps mounted against the auditorium's limestone wall.

The hemicycle formed by the curve of the Ariel Rios Building was to be complemented by a similarly curved facade to be built across the street on the site of the Old Post Office Building.

The burnished aluminum and brass staircase balustrade is consistent with Arthur Brown's designs throughout the Departmental Auditorium.

The center of the curved facade of the Ariel Rios Building along Twelfth Street is marked by an Ionic colonnaded pavilion. The tympanum sculpture by Adolph Alexander Weinman is entitled *The Spirit of Civilization and Progress.*

Inspired by the Place Vendôme in Paris, the hemicycle was
intended by the architects of this building, William Adams
Delano and William T. Aldrich, to be a central feature of
the Federal Triangle plan.

The interior hallways follow the curve of the hemicycle.

The sidewalk arcade of the hemicycle is laid with flagstone,
and the original globe lighting fixtures have been replaced
with octagonally shaped lanterns.

In the north anteroom of the postmaster general's reception hall stand six aluminum statues of postal delivery men set in niches. The *Alaska Snowshoe Mail Carrier* was sculpted by Chaim Gross and the *Hawaiian Postman* was done by Louis Slobodikin.

The floor of the postmaster general's reception room is covered in dark green and white-veined marble and surrounded by butternut paneling. Overhead three huge chrome and glass prism chandeliers hang from the coffered ceiling.

Reginald Marsh's murals of the mail being transferred from an ocean liner to a harbor mail boat cover the wall in the north elevator lobby of the fourth floor.

The balustrade is cast bronze with balusters of two ribbed posts alternating with a single post decorated with twisted serpents.

A prominent feature of the Ariel Rios Building is a seven-story spiral marble staircase. In the center of the spiral a chandelier hangs from the ceiling of the seventh floor. It has exposed bulbs to illuminate each floor and culminates in a chrome and brass globe.

The Bureau of Alcohol, Tobacco, and Firearms occupies the
southern third of the Ariel Rios Building.

An ornate lantern marks the entrance through the hemicycle's arcade to the Ariel Rios Building.

The Federal Trade Commission Building was the last Triangle building to be completed; it was designed by the architectural firm of Bennett, Parsons, and Frost and was finished in 1938.

On the south side of the Federal Trade Commission Building along Constitution Avenue, the doorway is covered with an aluminum grille designed by William McVey and surmounted by a bas-relief panel depicting foreign trade sculpted by Carl Ludwig Schmitz.

Looking west, the Federal Trade Commission Building sits at the point where Constitution and Pennsylvania avenues cross. As evidenced by the Federal Trade Commission Building, L'Enfant's plan for Washington, D.C., dictated acutely angled building lots, which provided both problems and opportunities for architects.

The apex of the Federal Triangle is marked by a fountain
built in 1950 to commemorate former secretary of the treasury and patron of the National Gallery of Art, Andrew
Mellon. This elegant fountain helps the Federal Trade
Commission Building turn the corner between Constitution
and Pennsylvania avenues.

Symbolic of guardianship, dogs (the sculptor's pets were used as models) are portrayed in the pediment of the National Archives Building's Constitution Avenue facade.

As designed by architect John Russell Pope, the National
Archives Building does not conform to many of the architectural standards of the other Federal Triangle buildings.
For example, it violates the uniform setbacks established in
the other buildings.

The south facade of the National Archives Building faces
Constitution Avenue and is the public entrance to the Dec-
laration of Independence and Bill of Rights exhibition.

On either side of the National Archives Building's Constitution Avenue entrance sit the enthroned figures *Heritage*
and *Guardianship* sculpted by James E. Fraser.

Designed by Zantzinger, Borie, and Medary, the Department of Justice Building was constructed on the site originally planned for the National Archives Building by the Commission of Fine Arts.

The northwest corner of the Justice Building at Tenth Street and Pennsylvania Avenue. The building was completed in 1934.

A view looking west from the Justice Building to the
Departmental Auditorium illustrates the uninterrupted
uniform cornice line along Constitution Avenue.

Above the doorway to the Justice Building's main entrance
is a bas-relief limestone panel designed by C. Paul Jennewein, upon which is inscribed, "Everything is created by
law and order."

The main entrance to the Department of Justice Building is
on the south facade along Constitution Avenue.

Eighteen aluminum torchères designed by Jennewein surround the Justice Building.

An aluminum-based fountain was placed in the middle of
the Great Court in the Department of Justice Building.

From the Tenth Street vehicular entrance to the Justice
Building the Great Court and fountain are visible. Most of
the courtyards of the Federal Triangle buildings are used as
makeshift parking lots.

Over one thousand of these colorful terra-cotta antefixes
decorate the roof of the Justice Building.

The exposed polychromatic aggregate ceiling was devised and cast by John Joseph Earley for the vehicular entrance portals to the Justice Building courtyard.

The Great Hall, on the second floor of the Department of Justice Building, accommodates lecture audiences of up to four hundred. The twelve-and-one-half-foot statues, *Spirit of Justice* and *Majesty of Law,* were designed by C. Paul Jennewein and cast in aluminum.

Egyptian motifs such as the lotus leaf are frequently used on the aluminum railing and ceiling of the stairwell behind the Great Hall.

In the Justice Building law library on the fifth floor, the murals painted by Maurice Sterne are entitled, *The Search for Truth*. One of a pair of aluminum lamps by C. Paul Jennewein appears in the foreground.

Jennewein modeled symbols of the four seasons on the
aluminum supports of his lamps in the Justice law library.

The attorney general's conference room is lined with American walnut paneling, the oil painting *Justice Triumphant* in the lunette above the room was done by Leon Kroll.

Murals by Henry Varnuum Poor representing themes associated with crime and the deliverance of justice line the
hallway outside the attorney general's offices.

The Fifteenth Street facade of the Department of Commerce stretches almost three city blocks but is partially masked by trees and relieved by four pedimented pavilions that jut out from the building. In 1934, at the time of its construction, this was the largest office building in the world. Louis Ayres of the York and Sawyer firm was the architect of the Commerce Building and a member of the Commission of Fine Arts.

Artist Boardman Roberts painted *Great Codifiers of the Law* for the stairwell and entrance to the Great Hall.

One of four pediments on the Fifteenth Street facade, this pediment contains a tympanum sculpture by James E. Fraser depicting the work of fishermen.

A sculpture by James E. Fraser entitled *Mining* is set into one of the pediments along the Fifteenth Street side of the Commerce Building.

133

The southern facade of the Commerce Building faces Constitution Avenue and is nineteen bays long with twelve
single columns and two sets of paired columns.

Along the Fourteenth Street facade, the exterior wall of the
building is recessed several feet behind the colonnade of
twenty-four fluted Doric columns.

Monumental neoclassical urns carved from granite flank the doorways of the Commerce Building along Constitution Avenue.

This Fifteenth Street entrance to the Commerce Building has inscribed above the door a quote attributed to George Washington.

The open grille of these bronze gates is foliated and crowned with patriotic eagle emblems.

Lit from behind by the sun, bronze gates hang in the drive-
way portals of the Department of Commerce Building.

Bronze chandeliers hang from the wonderful gold painted
and glazed ceiling of the main entry lobby on Fourteenth
Street.

Ornate bronze doors grace the Department of Commerce
Building's entrance lobby elevators.

141

The secretary of commerce's office as occupied by Secretary of Commerce Robert Mosbacher.

The law library (formerly known as the Old Patent Office Library) occupies the northwest corner of the first floor of the Commerce Building. The piers are clad in American walnut and the groin vaults are painted with foliate borders.

From east to west a corridor one hundred and sixty-eight feet long runs nearly the width of the building from the Fourteenth Street lobby to the Fifteenth Street side of the Commerce Building.

144

The richness of materials used in the Commerce Department is exhibited in the Fourteenth Street lobby where the
mosaic floor is made up of five different marbles and the
groin-vaulted ceiling of the lobby's vestibule is gilded.

The first- through seventh-floor offices overlook this courtyard—one of six courtyards in the Commerce Building.

A keystone sculpted head is placed in the arched passage
to the lobby vestibule.

View from the Ariel Rios Building across the Great Plaza to the Fourteenth Street facade of the Department of Commerce Building.

The neoclassical attic story of the Commerce Building is decorated with owls, eagles, fruit swags, and ribbon festoons carved in limestone.

There are twenty-seven bays along the Constitution Avenue facade of the Internal Revenue Service Building, with three central arches marking the building's entrance.

The Internal Revenue Service Building at Tenth Street and Constitution Avenue was designed by Louis Simon and constructed between 1929 and 1930.

The Internal Revenue Service was the first of the Triangle buildings to be built; but as it was to house an ancillary bureau rather than a department, the building is one of the simplest in the Triangle.

The northwestern section of the Internal Revenue Service
Building has a modified mansard roof that matches the roof
of the Ariel Rios Building across Tenth Street. In the background the Romanesque style Old Post Office Building
occupies the site that was originally intended for the rest of
the Internal Revenue Service Building.

SELECT BIBLIOGRAPHY

Bennett, Edward H. Diaries. In the office of Edward H. Bennett, Jr., Chicago.

Brown, Glenn. *Memories, 1860–1930.* Washington, D.C.: W. F. Roberts, 1931.

Brown, Glenn, ed. *Improvement of the City of Washington, D.C.* Washington, D.C.: Government Printing Office, 1901.

Coontz, John Leo. "L'Enfant's Dream of Washington Coming True." *American City* 38 (February 1928): 79–81.

Cox, William V., ed. *Celebration of the 100th Anniversary of the Establishment of the Seat of Government in the District of Columbia.* Washington, D.C.: Government Printing Office, 1901.

Delano, William Adams. "A Letter from Mr. William Adams Delano." *Federal Architect* (January/April 1943): 19.

Embury, Aymar. Review of *Daniel H. Burnham*, by Charles Moore. *Literary Review*, December 3, 1921.

Grant, Ulysses S., III. "The L'Enfant Plan and Its Evolution." *Columbia Historical Society Records* 33–34 (1932): 1–23.

———. "The New City of Washington." *Review of Reviews and World's Work* 86 (November 1932): 33–35.

Hale, William Harlan. "The Grandeur That Is Washington." *Harper's Monthly Magazine* 168 (April 1934): 560–69.

James, Harlean. "Architectural Control Now a Fact in Washington." *American City* 43 (July 1930): 148.

———. "The Washington Triangle Rises." *Review of Reviews and World's Work* 91 (January 1935): 61–62.

McKee, Oliver, Jr. "Washington Rebuilt." *Commonweal* (June 9, 1933): 154–55.

Moore, Charles. *Daniel H. Burnham.* 2 vols. Boston: Houghton Mifflin, 1921.

———. *Development of the United States Capital.* Washington, D.C.: Government Printing Office, 1930.

———. "The Government and the Practicing Architect." *Journal of the American Institute of Architects* 16 (March 1928): 90–93.

———. "The Government's Architectural Tradition." *Federal Architect* (January 1934): 8–11.

———, ed. *The Improvement of the Park System of the District of Columbia.* Washington, D.C.: Government Printing Office, 1902.

———. *The Life and Times of Charles Follen McKim.* Boston: Houghton Mifflin, 1929.

———. *Memoirs.* 3 vols. *Records of the Commission of Fine Arts,* Record Group 66, Charles Moore Papers. National Archives.

———. Papers. Manuscript Division, Library of Congress.

———. "Personalities in Washington Architecture." *Columbia Historical Society Records* 37–38 (1937): 1–15.

———. *The Promise of American Architecture.* Washington, D.C.: American Institute of Architects, 1905.

———. "Speech to the Washington Society of Fine Arts," February 18, 1937. Reprinted in *Congressional Records,* March 1, 1937, 75th Cong. 1st Sess. H.R. appendix, 371–73.

———. "Standards of Taste." *American Magazine of Art* 21 (July 1930): 365–67.

———. "The Transformation of Washington." *National Geographic* 43 (June 1923): 569–96.

———. "Washington as a Center of Culture." *Records of the Commission of Fine Arts,* Record Group 66, General Correspondence. National Archives.

———. "Washington—City of Splendor." *Current History* 32 (May 1930): 249–56.

———. *Washington: Past and Present.* New York: Century, 1929.

"National Capital Park and Planning Commission." *American City* 35 (July 1926): 103.

Newman, Oliver P. "Uncle Sam's Housing Problem." *Review of Reviews and World's Work* 73 (January 1926): 80–86.

Peaslee, Horace W. "The Federal City Planning Commission." *American City* 33 (August 1925): 188–89.

Pond, Irving K. "The American Architect." *Architectural Review* (December 7, 1921): 417–20.

Shurtleff, Arthur A. "Guiding the Growth of the City of Washington." *American City* 33 (July 1925): 40–41.

Simon, Louis A. "Development of Proposed Federal Building Group at Washington." *Journal of the American Institute of Architects* 16 (February 1928): 61–63.

"Two Notable American Art Commissions." *American City* 39 (November 1928): 131.

Watson, Forbes. "The Innocent Bystander." *American Magazine of Art* 28 (June 1935): 371–74.

Wilson, Otto. "Washington's Big Building Program." *Review of Reviews and World's Work* 74 (November 1926): 497–504.

Zangrando, Joanna Schneider. "Monumental Bridge Design in Washington, D.C., as a Reflection of American Culture: 1886 to 1932." Ph.D. diss., George Washington University, 1974.

INDEX